"Uncle Jamie" and Me

Jack Jordan

*Skip & Del,
Hope you like it!
Lucky*

The Author, Aunt Vera, and Uncle Jamie
Gribble's Grocery, 891 Traction St., Clarksburg, WVA
1950 or '51

"Uncle Jamie" and Me

Jack Jordan

PROTEA

© Copyright 2001 Jack Jordan. All rights reserved.

Uncle Jamie and Me
Jack Jordan

ISBN 1-883707-80-3

Protea Publishing
Atlanta Georgia USA

email: kaolink@msn.com
web site: www.proteapublishing.com

Introduction

Everything I have written herein is according to what I have heard or as I remember it first hand. So if any surviving member of the family wishes to take issue with any of it please keep it to yourself. Unless of course, you were present.

I can only attest to the truth of those events that I was personally involved in and pass on information as it was told to me by others. I must also confess to the employment of a smattering of literary license in order to transition certain events, and to be perfectly honest, to spice up an otherwise mundane experience or activity. I must also confess a lack of control where I interject my disappointment in the changes in attitudes we have experienced since I was a boy.

Also, the incident, activity and outcome have always been more important to me than the specific date or time frame so the reader will have to bear with that generality.

Chapter One

One of my earliest recollections of "Uncle Jamie" was as a small boy in the early 1930's wandering into his bedroom in Clarksburg, West Virginia where I saw his blood stained suit laying on his bed and heard the sound of him taking a shower. Later, my grandmother told me that another car had run his car off of a mountain road and one of his friends who had been with him had been killed.

Another recollection was when he promised me a present if I spent the night with him and aunt Vera when I wanted to go home and be with my mother, who was his sister. The truth of the matter, I found out when I was older, was that he was out all afternoon and evening with a bunch of his cronies and didn't get home 'till late and didn't want to make the drive to take me home after aunt Vera had taken care of me that afternoon. The next day I was taken downtown and they bought me a pedal car which was a very expensive toy by the day's standards. I must have torn up at least three or four of those cars before I got too big for them. I would pile every kid in the neighborhood in and on those cars until sometimes they broke or ruptured. One time, I had so many kids on the car, the wheels actually flew off in different directions. Another time I had so many kids on it that I couldn't negotiate a turn at the bottom of a hill at the corner of Main and Monticello and smashed it into a telephone pole.

"Uncle Jamie" got a big kick out of that and would just take me downtown and buy me another one when I broke one beyond repair.

This did not set too well with my mother of course, who was a very practical woman and did not believe that a child should be taught irresponsibility intentionally, especially hers! It wasn't the first time "Uncle Jamie" didn't see eye to eye with my mother, and other family members as well.

In fact they did not just disagree about some things, they disagreed about how to live, work, and play. He seemed to be at odds with anyone who believed you should work physically hard for an honest living and since most of my relatives did just that he went his way and they went theirs. He told me that once when he was young he went to work for my dad who was a mason, and was given a "hod" which was a tool designed to carry brick, manually, to the masons laying brick on the walls of the building. He said that it didn't take him long to find out that it wasn't comfortable in his hands, was not his "cup of tea", and he threw the hod as far out in the woods as he could and walked home.

The fact that they went their separate ways didn't mean they didn't care about each other; it just meant they accepted the way he was and didn't make any more of it than was necessary. Most were blue-collar people who were busy trying to make ends meet through a very hard economical period in our country's history. In fact, most of the family visited him regularly during the time he spent in state prison. Sometimes they would take a basket of food and make a picnic out of the visit.

My family very seldom made too much of anything. They all didn't have too much to say and usually got right to the point. I found this to be true with most of that generation and area culture. They were doers, not too prone to a lot of talking. My father was an unusually quiet man who felt he had talked too much after answering a few questions seriously so he began to make a joke out of the conversation or the question. His response to anything he considered too serious was to twist it in a humorous way which was his way, I think to say, lighten up, or get lost! The only offhand remark he ever made about my uncle was that he was certainly different and that he was the only man he ever knew who got out of bed in the middle of the day and looked for a couch. Thinking back, I now suspect that my dad was one of the few men my uncle respected and did not want to cross if he could avoid it. Once when my mother and my sister and I were visiting he got drunk one night and roughed up my mother when my grandmother asked her to try and get him to go to bed. When he apologized to my mother the next day he asked her to not mention it to my dad.

At that time I had no idea what he did for a living and didn't give it much thought. I heard that he drank and gambled almost every night and later on also heard that he was a man to "step away from," as they used to say in the mountains, when he was angry. He was what they called in those days a "hellraiser". He was a rebel who seemed to enjoy the risk of living on the edge. In spite of his generosity and sense of humor he had a mean streak and relished teasing until the object of his teasing would be on the verge of tears or striking out.

Once, he had me so angry I lowered my head and charged him with my fists swinging. He protected himself by simply placing his hand on the top of my head and holding me off until I wore myself out, lost my balance, and fell down while he laughed so hard he almost pissed his pants. At least, that is what he told my dad. Another time he teased me to the point that my grandmother went after him with her favorite weapon, which was her broom. I noticed that he didn't laugh when she did.

Later on he told me that in the future when I had to fight to "make every punch count" and "wait until I could get to 'em and not waste energy on hittin' air"! But he stressed "talkin' and or walkin" if you could pull it off.

He called me "Britchy" which was short for britches-broke-down. The reason was because when I was little my pants with the button up flap in the back was hanging down quite often. So, I became

"Britchy" for as long as he was alive. No one else in the family ever called me that but him. Once in a while some kid would try but my reaction wasn't worth the privilege whether I won the fight or not. I was taught early on that there was no shame in losing as long as they weren't eager to try you again. My dad always said to "make sure you get a couple sandwiches while they were getting lunch."

My uncle was a complex, generous, sometimes brooding son of a bitch with a mean streak but he was my favorite uncle because he was a complex, generous, sometimes brooding son of a bitch with a mean streak.

Early in his youth he decided to take issue with the government over the right to make, sell, and drink liquor, and became involved in the subsequent activities that followed when you decided to actively pursue that belief. It is a matter of record that quite a few people made that decision at that time.

This was long before he married his first wife who died from the influenza epidemic eighteen months after she bore him a son, James, or Jimmy as he was called and who was raised by my grandmother. I can't remember just exactly when Aunt Vera officially became my aunt. I only know that they dated and maybe lived together off and on quite awhile until they decided to get married. Aunt Vera was a very attractive red head with a great sense of humor who went to my defense with "Unc" and a few other family members more than once over a few situations

I wandered into. I remember one of her comments as, "Well, that's an amusing little situation you've got yourself into!"

She and my uncle never had children. I never knew why and no one ever mentioned it to my knowledge. Maybe he figured one kid was enough!

Cousin Jim, and his father did not seem to have a good relationship, "Uncle Jamie" was a classic do-as-I-say and not-as-I-do father and I can remember many good word fights when I was little and Jimmy was still in high school. One of the most serious was when Jimmy decided he was going to quit school in his senior year. He and "Unc" almost came to blows over that one and Jimmy stayed in school just long enough to graduate from high school which was a shame because if anyone belonged in college and beyond, it was Jimmy. Once, Jimmy left home and was picked up by the sheriff while hitch-hiking through a little town in Georgia. The sheriff contacted "Uncle Jamie" who sent the sheriff bus fare to send Jimmy home but only after he worked him awhile on the road crew. After awhile the sheriff put Jimmy on a bus with instructions from "Unc" for the bus driver not to let him off of the bus until they reached Clarksburg. I don't know if Jimmy ever forgave his father for that. Maybe he knew, and remembered the story about "Unc" being sent to the train station to pick up the overcoat his father, our grandfather, had left there. It seems that he retrieved the coat, sold it, and didn't return home until he had spent all of the money. None of us ever learned of the eventual consequences of that event!

During the years I was growing up I can't remember seeing the two of them together very often and cannot say whether they reconciled prior to "Uncle Jamie's" death. Cousin Jim and my cousin Glen, two of my favorite people, never had a critical word during my so-called foot-loose and fancy-free years. They never hesitated to open the door and point to the couch whenever I showed up in the middle of the night. Jim's wife Lucille was always there to fix coffee and sandwiches during our all-night poker games. Glen's wife, Frankie, was a born caregiver, and my Dad always said she was an "Angel" in human form! I was always made to feel "at home" in both houses during the time that I didn't have one and basically lived out of the trunk of my car!

"Uncle Jamie also had a brother, Uncle Lee. I don't believe I ever heard a word, much less a kind word, from either one of them about the other when I was growing up. In fact, when I was older, I stopped visiting my Uncle Lee for any length of time because eventually he got around to "bad mouthing" his brother.

"Uncle Jamie" was a hard man and as they say in the vernacular, it was his way or the highway, right up until the day he died.

Chapter Two

Most of my memories of "Uncle Jamie" were from the time I was four or five until thirteen or fourteen years old. During those years my mother would send me to spend the summer with him and Aunt Vera. My maternal grandmother also stayed with them at that time when she wasn't with us or my mother's sister, Aunt Edith. When I think about why my mother sent me to spend the summers with "Uncle Jamie" it was probably to get me off of the streets of Washington DC, while school was out. We didn't live in the worst neighborhoods, but we didn't live in the best either. My mother must have figured that Aunt Vera and Grandma were there to offset any negative exposure to my uncle. My family had moved to the DC area during the depression because that was where my father found work as a brickmason.

"Uncle Jamie" had bought what was known as a "roadhouse" on state route #50 in a valley about three miles down the mountain from the small village of Mount Storm, West Virginia. It was a gas station/restaurant/dance floor/bar combination that included owner's living quarters on the second floor with individual cabins on the property that were for rent to travelers. It was located in an area of mostly small and medium sized farms with one or two large dairy farms along the main highway. A number of small mining towns were located up in the mountains some distance from the highway but although they had the usual company store, many of the miners still frequented the roadhouse, especially on Saturday nights.

He acquired the property soon after he was released from prison and it was an obvious change of pace from his previous lifestyle. The bar was licensed for beer and wine only but he always had homemade liquor on hand and entertained short visits from friends and sometimes even local law enforcement people in the back room. Of course the liquor in the back room was free.

The story goes that he bought the property with a sum of money he received from a former partner in the liquor business after he was released from prison. Why his partner felt he was obligated for the money we can only guess.

Chapter Three

My "sidekick" during the summers I spent in the mountains was a pit bull/boxer mix dog named Trooper which my uncle had entered in the fighting pits until he had grown too old. He retired undefeated and became a valuable member of the family. My uncle called him "Doodlebug" sometimes, for some unknown reason, and "Monk" because he sat like a monkey up against the counter in the roadhouse. But he was always just Trooper to me.

We were inseparable and he was my partner in many exciting boyhood adventures together. He was a big one hundred pounds plus of fawn colored muscle with a big broad forehead and intelligent brown eyes. His body was covered with the battle scars that were evidence of his time in the pits against all comers, but to me he was beautiful. He went everywhere I went if he possibly could, many times against the objections of my uncle even though he knew the consequences of punishment when he got back home.

No matter where I was going, he was usually right behind me, beside me or in front of me foraging in the brush and if I was carrying the 22 single shot rifle, my uncle could whistle all he wanted but it was to no avail. Trooper would fade into the woods until we were a good distance away from the house and then appear next to me for the rest of our outing. It was like he was an ostrich. Even though he could hear my uncle, it was okay because he couldn't be seen, or something like that. If I had that rifle nothing short of locking or tying him up could stop him from going with me.

Trooper was absolutely fearless and almost human in understanding what the danger was and who might be harmed. He also was more on guard when I didn't have the rifle. During the summers I spent in the mountains he protected me from all types of wildlife.

When my uncle gave me the rifle and taught me how to shoot out behind the roadhouse, he would give me a certain number of bullets. When I had fired all of the bullets at a makeshift target he had set up he would come check out the target and then take the rifle and put it away.

After a period of time when, I suspect that, he figured I was good enough, he would give me a certain number of bullets and tell me that I was to bring home that number of squirrels or rabbits for stew which my Aunt Vera or grandmother would make. I am sure he always gave me one or two extra bullets to allow for a miss or two, but I very seldom missed.

I would shoot the squirrels or rabbits and Trooper would retrieve them after a few shakes to make sure they were dead. Of course, my uncle had taught me to go for the head shot so it was a clean kill and dressing them out did not require cleaning out bullet residue.

It was during some of these times that I was scared shitless, not only for myself but mostly for Trooper. As stated earlier, he would attack anything that he felt was a threat and much of the wildlife we came upon, that was capable of injuring someone, became aggressive when startled. It was only natural that they would do so but Trooper never hesitated. His altercations were mostly with snakes, and he paid the price more than once going after rattlers and moccasins.

Whoever decided to have a rattlesnake pictured on the West Virginia State flag probably didn't intend to point out how very much at home in those mountains they are, but believe me they were not in short supply at those times! I can remember once seeing a coiled snake on the white line, in the middle of the road, part of it flattened where it had been run over by a car or truck, still striking at the tires of a car as it drove by.

Like I said, old Trooper paid the price a few times when he went after snakes and even when he was struck he would finish the snake off. Then he would be gone for anywhere from three to five days.

When Trooper came home he would be gaunt and covered with a mix of dried mud and clay. My uncle said that he would find a bog of that stuff and lay in it until he was over the snake bite. How that helped him I have never been able to find out. He was laid up a whole lot longer when he went at it with a bobcat and almost "bought the farm" when we came up on a medium size black bear in a blackberry patch. That bear would slap Trooper and roll him until Trooper couldn't hardly move anymore and finally seemed to listen to me calling him off. He ended up standing off from the bear with his tongue hanging out, bleeding from cuts and gashes all over his body, and growling with each labored exhale of breath while the bear lumbered off as if he was bored with the whole affair. Trooper was so stove up that I had to go and get the wheelbarrow to cart him home. I was always afraid that my uncle would be angry with me for letting Trooper get into those scrapes but when I asked him why he didn't, he replied that he knew the dog and knew that he was difficult to control when he was faced with another menacing animal of any kind. He added that if any one could control him it would be me, besides himself, of course. I always felt a little proud of that!

Uncle Jamie would scold him when he came home from one of these adventures anyway, and Trooper would hide under the kitchen table until things quieted down.

But he was always ready to go when I started off with the 22.

Chapter Four

Not much happened at the roadhouse during the week except for a traveler now and then and routine business from the local farmers, truckers and coal miners who came in for gas and or groceries. The economy was slow, so business was slow. Sometimes a friend of my uncle's would drop in for a visit on the way to Clarksburg, Fairmont, or the other way, over and down the mountain to Keyser.

Usually, before they left they were afforded the hospitality of the back pantry where "Unc" kept his homemade liquor.

All kinds of people stopped in for a visit including state and local officials and after awhile it was not surprising to see an occasional deputy sheriff or even a state trooper drop by. It was the Sheriff or the local deputy, I don't remember which, that was an old friend of my uncle's, who ate lunch at the roadhouse at least once a week, sometimes for dinner, bringing his wife and two grown boys. Aunt Vera would sit and visit with them during those times and I never saw him pick up a check or pay for one.

The story goes that it was the "Feds" that put "Unc" in the state prison at Elkins. He had too many friends on the state and local level and if the "Feds" had stayed out of it he would not have been arrested and convicted.

The type of people that came by for a visit sure did give some support to that story!

Friday and Saturday nights were another story altogether! It was a classic "Katy bar the door" situation. The farmers, truckers and miners showed up to settle up for credit extended and for a good time, and most of them acted as if they didn't get drunk, dance with all the women and fight someone, or just anyone, it was a lost time. Years later when I would hear a song by either one of the two Hanks, Snow or Williams, I would think of the roadhouse on Friday and Saturday nights.

"Uncle Jamie" and Trooper usually headed things off before too many people got into it. "Unc" would speak Troopers name and point and the dog would approach the man that "Unc" had pointed to quickly, and stare at him with a low growl. He would stand in that position until he was called off, and he was not called off until the man assured "Unc" that he would not make trouble.

Once in a while some guy would think he could handle Trooper but that was a big mistake. All my uncle had to say was "get him" and Trooper would charge in low, grab one leg and start dragging. He would drag the man around the floor until my uncle called him off. Usually by the time he was called off the man was in no condition to walk much less cause trouble.

There were also a few level heads that would give a hand when necessary because most of them knew my uncle would take care of the situation in a more serious manner if it continued to escalate.

He had demonstrated his ability with a pistol out behind the roadhouse a few times. He and my Dad, who I felt was an expert with a pistol, would have shooting contests when my parents came up to drop me off or pick me up. Both of them could keep a tin can in the air, shooting from the hip with either hand, until the gun was empty.

My dad was just a hair more accurate than my uncle but the difference was not enough to bet hard money on any given day.

However, the word throughout the mountain was enough to earn them respect as well as attract wannabe shooters who soon found out that the kind of shooting my uncle and dad did was not easily matched. They were not trick shooters nor fast draw artists. They were quick, accurate, cool, and consistent which my dad explained was necessary if you ever had to defend yourself in a gunfight. There were many good rifle shots in the mountains and some were just as accurate as my dad and uncle but it was general knowledge that a handgun was more effective in a close or crowded situation.

Guns were one of the tools that a family had in those days, and especially in the mountains where people hunted for most of their meat and relied on them for protection because the law was usually a good distance away. Accidents, involving guns in the home, were unheard of in those days, because I think, they were family tools, and everyone was aware of their purpose and the danger in handling them. From the time they were little, they were taught how to use, clean, repair, and store them safely. The family rules concerning these tools were respected by all family members. The present day hysteria over guns is I believe, due partly to our loss of respect for authority! No weapon in the world ever did any damage until the human element was introduced.

But the law and his two boys usually arrived in record time when things got out of hand at the roadhouse. He was an average size man, although well proportioned physically, but his two boys were six foot plus weighing over two hundred pounds each.

When things erupted too fast for my uncle and Trooper to keep a lid on them Aunt Vera would telephone and the law and his two sons would pull up in a flat bed truck with what looked like a jail cell built on the back. One son would position himself at the front door and one would stand at the back door while the father would go in the front door with what looked like an ax handle.

Soon people began to exit the roadhouse in an obvious hurry with my uncle, Trooper, and the law sorting things out. The ladies were allowed to leave with no interference but the men were collared and thrown into the back of the truck with the jail cell on it. I don't remember hearing any of the ladies complaining about not being included in the back of the truck. Every man that the boys could grab went into the cell until the brawl was over. After that, my uncle would point out the trouble makers and the others would be let out of the cell. The remaining ones spent the night in the cell and paid the law three dollars apiece to be let out the next morning. The ones who did not have the three dollars were transported to the nearest jail to wait for the next circuit court judge to hear their case. Usually by the time the judge showed up they were let go for time served and a small court cost. Quite a few ended up waiting for the judge because three dollars was a lot of money in those days.

As a small boy who enjoyed all kinds of adventure, I looked forward to Saturday nights. I would sit at the top of the stairs to the second floor with Trooper until my uncle called him down. I would then sneak down the stairs to watch until my aunt would call for the law. I would then go back up stairs and watch out the window when the two sons would be grabbing the men when they came out of the roadhouse and throwing them into the back of the truck.

It was a lot of excitement for a boy of my age and my mother never mentioned whether she knew about those times or not.

Of course my dad did mention once, in his dry mountain "twang," that I was getting a real "squared" education. I never did find out what each side of the square represented although I have had a few ideas over the years.

Chapter Five

The first summer I spent with "Unc" and Aunt Vera was pretty normal for a boy in the country except for a few turn of events. I played with two boys in a family that lived down the road and one boy who lived on a farm across the road up on the mountain.

We did the kind of things you would expect boys our age to do. Most of the time the two boys in the family and I played together. "Big D" and "Little D" were the only two boys in the family and were called that because they were both named after their daddy but had different middle names. Of course, the family called them by their middle names. My uncle referred to them as Pete and Repeat.

The rest of the kids in the family were all girls and they didn't play with us boys much except big "D" would tease them about sneaking up and watching them put their bathing suits on in the bushes and they would get mad and threaten to "tell Mama".

We hunted and picked blackberries in the woods and fished and swam in the river. We also investigated old abandoned sheds and small houses in the remote areas of the woods. Most of them were located along or close to the river. Picking blackberries and swimming in the river was when we usually ran into snakes, rattlers in the woods and moccasins in the river.

Trooper would sit on the bank of the river and guard us kids and that is when he killed more than one moccasin who, whether it was a danger to us kids or not made the mistake of dropping out of the overhanging brush and swimming towards one of us. Trooper would rush into the water, grab the snake, carry it out of the water and finish it off on the bank of the river.

One of our most popular activities was playing fort and mock war battles in the northwest corner of a cow pasture between the roadhouse and the bridge crossing the river. A huge pile of wood shavings had been dumped there by a local mill and had become almost a small mountain that we could dig tunnels into.

Before the summer was over we had dug a network of tunnels and rooms throughout that pile of wood shavings and had numerous battles with cow pie as ammunition.

Uncle Jamie cleaned me up outside with the garden hose and a stiff brush more than once after I came home from one of the more serious battles. He claimed that I smelled like the "south end of a flu stricken horse goin' north". He was going to make me eat dinner outside until I "aired out" but grandma and Aunt Vera put a stop to that.

Another thing that happened that summer was a very pleasant surprise.

Almost every day an old man who I only knew as Mr. Ty would come walking down out of the mountains on the dirt road that intersected with route #50 next to the wood shaving pile. He would arrive at the roadhouse at about mid-morning and sit on one of the steps in the front, whittle wood with his knife and spit tobacco juice out in the driveway. He would spend most of the day, almost everyday except Sundays, until early afternoon, when he would get, up throw his hand up in a farewell gesture and begin his walk back down the road and up the mountain. (Aunt Vera would bring him a sandwich and a beer for lunch.) I remember a friend of my uncle's asking why he didn't run the old bum off?

My uncle replied that there was a second set of steps into the building, the tobacco juice kept the bugs busy, and the old bum owned that mountain that he lived on.

I don't believe Mr. Ty ever said more than a few words to me at one time and those times were very few. He talked with my uncle more than anyone though I never knew what about. But I was not much interested at my age. I would catch him watching me now and then with a little grin, but when he noticed me looking at him he would go back to his whittling and spitting.

Every now and then a truck full of ponies would stop for gas while passing through on their way to the coalmines. Ponies were used to pull the carts on the rail tracks in and out of the coalmines in those days. They may still do it for all I know. Quite a few times my uncle had called me out to show me the ponies and tease me about which one did I want him to buy for me. When I would point one out he would laugh and walk off. This happened more than once while Mr. Ty watched.

It was the next morning after one of these times that I was helping my uncle clean up in front of the roadhouse around the front where the gas pumps were and neither one of us noticed when Mr. Ty arrived. But, when we noticed him, he was standing just behind us with a brown and white pinto pony standing next to him. He had let the reins of the bridle drop to the ground while he tightened the cinch on the saddle.

My uncle didn't say a word when Mr. Ty handed me the reins and said that the pony was mine to "take care of and ride for the summer". He said that he would take care of him in the winter. Then he turned to my uncle and said, "Now you can find something else to tease that boy about Jim". My uncle laughed and said he guessed he would just have to do that.

The pony's name was "Socks" because he had four white feet and he and Trooper got along fine. Trooper was always ready to go when I saddled up Socks unless my uncle made him stay home for some reason. Mr. Ty always had Socks ready and waiting for me when I arrived for the next summer and didn't even seem to notice my uncle complaining about spoiling me more than he did.

Chapter Six

My uncle built a lean-to in back of the roadhouse for Socks, so, I think he felt justified when he gave me a hard time. In a way he was justified because from the time Mr. Ty brought Socks I was pretty hard to find and finally my grandmother had to remind me that I was expected to help out around the roadhouse.

I didn't miss much of the unpopulated parts of the valley riding Socks with Trooper tagging along. I don't think I could be called anti-social, but I really enjoyed those times during the summers I spent in the mountains with just Socks and Trooper. To this day I do not have to have someone around all the time and in fact, need a balance of time to myself. I attribute that to my childhood summers at Uncle Jamie's.

Most of my travels in the valley were along the river looking for good fishing spots. Socks would stand and graze with his reins on the ground for hours when I found a good spot. When Trooper was along he would find a shady place to stretch out and doze mostly with one eye open.

There were some great rainbow trout pools in that river, between the highway and an old abandoned mill, two, maybe three miles, from the highway. I most always brought home a mess of fish to the point where my aunt had to remind me that they liked other kinds of meat sometimes and the fish didn't keep too well in the icebox during the warm months.

"Big D" and I would sometime double up on Socks and go to a pool we knew about and "lasso" fish for sport. After we caught them we would let them go. "Big D" said he invented "lassoing" fish and I had no reason to doubt him. We would go along about dusk, just before the sun set, with "lassos" made out of fish wire and catch the fish dozing along the banks of the river. If you dropped the wire 'lasso" down easy into the water and let the fish float through you could snare him up and out of the water with a quick flip of the wrist. There were times we would spend all of the twilight hours at the river, until it was so dark you couldn't hardly see the river much less the fish.

Then I would drop "Big D" off at his house on the way home and walk Socks down the road until we came to the big oak tree that hung over the road, next to a small church, between his house and the roadhouse. The tree was full of bats and when you passed under the tree at night they would dive on you. I found it out one night when I was foot racing a rainstorm home and stopped under the tree to catch my breath. After that, and before I had Socks, I would run as fast as I could past the tree and more than once I could feel the air stir about my head when one almost made contact.

After I got Socks I would gallop him past the

tree as fast as he would go and be on the other side before they knew I was coming.

Incidentally, the church I mentioned was a brief attraction for us kids. I can't remember when services for the small congregation were held exactly but I do remember that it was at night. "Big D" decided that we should observe the services, some night, through the back window of the church, from the old cross-rail fence located there.

So, when the congregation gathered one night, unknown to them, we all sat on the back fence to watch the services.

They started off pretty normal with some announcements, some preaching about not letting the devil take you over, some singing, and some more preaching. As the service progressed it became louder and some of the congregation began to join in with verbal support for the preacher and some began to moan and fall on the floor until the whole congregation was moving in some way or verbally expressing themselves in some way and the preacher was yelling at the top of his voice to be heard over all of the noise and music.

I was taking it all in with my mouth hanging open the same as everyone else except "Big D" who by this time had fallen off of the fence twice and was at this point laying in the grass laughing so hard that we all didn't hear the man approach us from the church. How he knew we were there we never knew because he certainly couldn't have heard us over the noise from the church.

By the time we saw him it was too late and he reached over the fence, grabbed "Big D" by the "scruff" of the neck and picked him up as if he was a puppy. "Is that the devil I hear in you boy?" he asked. "Because if it is I will have to shake him out of you!". With that he demonstrated one good shake, dropped "Big D" on his feet, and then turned and walked back towards the church.

"Big D" hardly landed on his feet and us kids, including him, were moving in all directions. It took me twice as long to get home going up the mountain through the woods and then down to the rear of the roadhouse except straight down the road. I thought I could hear someone behind me all of the way.

Early the next morning Trooper stuck his nose in my face and woke me up. I rolled over and covered up with the blanket and told him to go away.

He was half way down the stairs when I heard my uncle say "I told you to go and get him up!". When I heard him coming back up the stairs I rolled over and covered myself up with my head under the blanket.

When I didn't respond to his nudging and whining he grabbed the blanket in his teeth and pulled me and the blanket out of bed so there wasn't anything left to do but get dressed and go down stairs to "face the music" as they used to say.

Sure enough, my uncle and a big guy with his collar on backward were sitting at one of the booths having a cup of coffee.

My uncle called me over and introduced me to the reverend who shook my hand with a firm but not abusive grip. After some polite conversation during which he asked me how I was enjoying my break from school and other niceties he stated that he would have to go. He rose to leave and then turned to me and said that next time my friends and I were welcome to join the congregation inside the church, especially if it was raining!

The look on my uncle's face promised non-religious retribution was forthcoming and a lesson in respect for other people's religious beliefs. These lessons came in the form of extra chores around the property for the rest of the summer.

Needless to say, none of us kids were interested in another service at the church. At least it didn't come up for discussion.

Chapter Seven

I got a little careless with snakes before that summer was over. It was like the old saying, "when it comes, it comes in bunches like bananas." I was struck by three different snakes that summer.

The first one was a big diamondback that I didn't hear because of the wind in the brush while I was sneaking up on some wild turkeys roosting in a tree on the other side of a crick my uncle said was one of the headwaters of the Potomac river. I had the 22 rifle and was concentrating on having turkey instead of fish, squirrel, or rabbit for a change. I had left Trooper home because I wasn't sure whether he would spook the birds before I could get a shot. Socks was grazing down the slope at the edge of the woods.

The snake hit me hard just above the heel of my boot and the last I saw of him was his tail disappearing under a bush. It was a good thing he decided to retreat because I was laying on the ground where he could have finished me off with a strike to the upper body.

I was so scared I could hardly think straight. I was afraid to look at where he struck me. All I could think of was that I should remain calm and get myself back home as soon as possible.

I picked up the rifle and for a brief moment wanted to find that son-of-a-bitch and shoot his head off but immediately thought better of it. I took my time going down the slope where Socks was grazing, climbed into the saddle and let him head towards the roadhouse. It seemed like an eternity until we arrived home with me feeling my foot swelling inside my boot and my leg beginning to go numb while the tears streamed down my face.

My grandmother saw me coming and sensed something was wrong and called for my uncle and aunt. They were all waiting when I rode up and after my uncle sorted out that I had been snake-struck he pulled me off of Socks and sat me on the picnic table. He began taking my boot off and at the same time told my aunt to get a sharp knife and some kitchen matches My grandmother kept telling me to stay calm because I kept asking if I was going to die. My uncle had removed my boot and was inspecting my foot when my aunt arrived with the knife and matches. I still could not look at where I was struck, I just knew that my foot was torn up. After inspecting my foot my uncle had picked the boot back up and was looking at it when he began to laugh. Of course my grandmother and aunt voiced their displeasure until he explained that the snake had not even pierced the boot through and in fact had left one fang on an angle imbedded just above the heel. He said that I must have moved in that split second that the snake struck so that it hit on the angle instead of straight on. My heel was not penetrated but did have a pretty good bruise from the force of the strike and being twisted at the same time. The swelling and numbness I felt was of course the result of the fear from the belief of being struck rather than actually being struck. Also, the boots I wore were made of thick leather that covered my leg to just below the knees and would have given pretty good protection even if the snake had struck me straight and solid. I kept that fang for quite a few years in a small box with some other "stuff" but I looked for it when I was home on leave from the service one time and was unable to find it.

The second incident was similar to the first but it was a water moccasin and no where as big as the rattler.

I was cutting across the field across the road from the roadhouse to go down to the wood shaving pile for one of our fort battles. There was a crick that wound through the field, under the old dirt road that went up into the mountain, and then emptied out into the river. Trooper was foraging off to the side and behind me and I had left Socks home because there were other animals in the field where the shaving fort was including mares and a stud stallion who would not treat Socks kindly.

Without looking I had stepped down on the bank of the crick and stepped right on a water moccasin. He had already coiled in reaction to my approach so that I inadvertently pinned a lot of him under my foot except enough of his head was free to strike into my boot more than once, and one last time just above my boot before Trooper had him behind the head. When Trooper grabbed him he almost tore the snake in half because I was still standing on him.

While Trooper carried what was left of him off I pulled up my dungarees and found two red rimmed small punctures just below my knee that were beginning to sting.

For some reason I didn't get as scared as I did the first time. Even though I knew that I had been hit this time I walked back to the roadhouse where "Uncle Jamie" cut a cross over top of each puncture and sucked out most of the venom. Then he and Aunt Vera put me in the truck and drove me to the veterinarian in Mt. Storm. The vet checked to make sure the wounds were still open and used some kind of a suction machine on them. After hearing the details he surmised that the snake had put most of his venom in my boot before he struck my leg.

He gave my aunt some drawing salve and said that if they didn't bring me back in a day or two he would know that I was all right. I did get a little feverish and had a sick stomach for a few days but after that I was back to normal.

The third time almost killed me! And, sometimes I think that the first two times instilled an attitude in me that caused the third time. In other words, I got cocky and thought that I didn't have to be real careful around snakes.

I had ridden Socks down to the river and left

him grazing next to a deep pool of water surrounded by big boulders while I fished from the top of one of them. Trooper had gone with "Uncle Jamie" somewhere and wasn't home when I left. I had fished for a while and caught a few trout, which were lying behind and to the right of me on the rock surface of the boulder I was sitting on. It was a drowsy afternoon and after awhile I laid back and closed my eyes with my fingers still on my line in the water. I don't know how much time had passed when I sensed movement where my fish were and sat up. When I did I caught actual movement out of the corner of my eye and turned my head to see what it was.

    I was surprised to find that the snake was attracted to my fish because I had no idea what they ate, but there was a water moccasin biting into one of the fish.

    I still can't believe what I did at that time. Without hesitation, and obviously without conscious thought, I flipped the back of my right hand at the snake and said, "get outta here!" The snake was stretched out but when I flipped my hand at it, it pulled its head back and struck me in the back of the hand.

    The shock of being struck didn't set in right away and I was mad. The snake began to slither off of the rock and I grabbed up a handful of stones and began to chase after it. After being hit by one of the stones more than once it hesitated at the river's edge, opened its mouth and a smaller snake exited from its mouth into the river ahead of the larger one. I remember wondering what that was all about but read later that they do eat other snakes.

At that point I realized that my hand was beginning to throb and what I was doing was only helping the poison to spread faster. By the time I reached Socks I was getting dizzy and my entire arm began to ache and tighten, I had difficulty getting up into the saddle. I hardly remembered the ride back to the roadhouse or when my uncle pulled me off of Socks. I was completely out of touch with everything for, I was told, five days and that I was not given much of a chance to survive at first. I was taken to the veterinarian again and while Aunt Vera stayed with me my uncle drove to Petersburg and brought an M.D. to back up the veterinarian. When I woke up my grandmother was sitting by my bed back at the roadhouse with tears in her eyes and as soon as I woke up she called for my aunt and uncle. Trooper was lying at her feet next to my bed.

My parents weren't told about the incident until I recovered and "Uncle Jamie" told my Dad that he would be willing to bet that the snake didn't survive. My mother didn't think that was funny.

Chapter Eight

One morning I was waiting to go with my uncle to Petersburg on business and watched the greyhound bus pull in front of the roadhouse while Trooper went to meet it. The bus delivered the weekly paper and sometimes a traveler would get off to visit a relative or friend in the valley or on the mountain. But the best part was that all of the drivers knew Trooper and they would not just open the door and throw the paper out in the driveway. They would hold the door open and Trooper would get on the bus and go all the way to the back wagging his tail to say hello to all of the passengers. Most of them got a big kick out of it and when Trooper had finished visiting with all of them the driver would give him the paper and he would get off the bus and take it to my grandmother.

The ironic part of all of this was that my grandmother always pretended that she didn't care for the dog but every now and then you would see her let her hand brush his coat when he went by and sometimes she would let him sit and lean against her until she felt someone was watching. But the bottom line was that no one got the paper but my grandmother and a few people found that out the hard way. None were bitten because the growl was clearly a serious warning, even when someone just wanted to read the headlines. They could just wait their turn after grandma was through with it.

Soon after Trooper had delivered the paper to my grandmother my uncle pulled his Dodge truck around and motioned for me to get in.

This is where I should explain a little bit about my uncle's driving philosophy. I think he believed that they shouldn't show that the car or truck would go that fast if they didn't want you to. And he usually drove from point A to point B just as fast as the car or truck would go except he did take mountain "hairpin" turns into consideration. But believe me the ride was still what you could call invigorating!

Petersburg is about 22 miles from Mt. Storm, which is about 3 miles from the roadhouse so we had about a 25 mile trip made up of mostly "hairpin" turns and steep grades to Petersburg.

Upon arriving in Petersburg the business trip consisted of about 20 minutes in the First Trust of West Virginia and the rest of the afternoon and evening in a saloon owned by a friend of my uncle's named Shorty. The saloon was a long narrow room with a bar that stretched from the front door to the back of the room where the kitchen and rest rooms were. A brass foot rail ran the length of the bar with a break now and then for a brass spittoon. Some booths, a few tables and chairs around a small dance floor, and a couple of pool tables in the back completed Shorty's bar. Shorty lived on the second floor and I never met a Mrs. Shorty so I guess he didn't have one.

I kind of liked to go on these trips with my uncle for a number of reasons, the first being that I could eat all I wanted from the lunch food on the bar that was available to customers for the price of a draft beer which I believe was a nickel at that time.

The second reason was that my uncle would let me have a beer later on in the evening which at my age usually put me to sleep pretty quick on one of the benches in the back of the bar. This of course gave my uncle the rest of the night to drink, play cards, and shoot pool with his buddies.

My uncle attracted women like flypaper attracted flies, so as soon as word got around that he was in town, women and men who enjoyed the evening atmosphere that he and his cronies created began to appear and join the party. It got pretty lively in Shorty's bar usually before I went down on the bench for the night and was just as exciting as the same kind of activity at the roadhouse.

But the most important reason that I liked the trips was that my uncle would not feel up to driving after pulling an "all niter" so he would let me drive. I could hardly see over the dash board and my feet barely reached the foot controls but "Unc" would bring along a couple of pillows for me to sit on and pull the seat up as far as it would go for me. He would drive out of town until we reached the city limits of Petersburg, and then I would drive from there to Mt. Storm where he would then drive down the mountain the last 3 miles to the roadhouse so that Aunt Vera and Grandma wouldn't know.

During my drive from Petersburg to Mt. Storm my uncle would "catnap" his hangover but wake up now and then to give me hell for going too fast and ask me if I thought I was "Barney Oldsfield." I didn't have a clue as to who Barney Oldsfield was or that he was a champion race car driver. But my uncle did have reason to tell me to slow down because as I gained confidence I would speed up on the straight sections of the road. Every now and then he would remind me to stay in my lane because the other one belonged to the guy coming the other way. Sometimes I would leave the car in second gear too long after topping out a steep grade resulting in him asking me if I planned to buy him a new gear box. However, I was very careful and slowed down on all of the "hairpin" curves because I always remembered the joke my dad told about how some of the turns in the mountains were so sharp that you should wear a catcher's mask to keep from sticking your nose up your ass.

But it was kind of ironic for my uncle to complain about how fast I was driving because of his driving reputation. One story was that, in his youth, he turned his car upside down on top of Kelly Hill outside of Clarksburg. No one, including him, could explain how he managed to do that although the one witness did point out that he went by pretty fast before it happened. No one could explain how he managed to climb out of the car without a scratch either, and there were no seat belts in those days.

My older cousin Glen told me about the time that "Unc" insisted on driving once when they were traveling from Washington DC to Clarksburg. Glen had just bought a used 1932 Chevy coupe and had reservations about letting "Unc" drive, which were justified when "Unc" put the accelerator to the floor and kept it there until the engine blew a rod coming down the mountain into the small village of Gormania. They took the Greyhound bus to Clarksburg while the one mechanic in Gormania repaired the car. Then Glen had to take the bus back to Gormania and pick up his car on the return trip to DC. He said that it was the last road trip he took with "Unc" and was glad that he never had to let him drive any one of his cars again!

In addition to the stories you heard and were told about his driving, many of the local gendarmes had first hand knowledge of his driving history from when he was in the liquor distribution business.

But under the circumstances, I understood why he was a little testy during the last return trip from Petersburg after the night in Shorty's bar. The fight broke out just before I fell asleep and the last thing I remember was "Uncle Jamie" explaining to a couple of his acquaintances from the Petersburg Police Department what went on and why he had to "calm the guy down" with a pool cue!

By the time we reached Mt. Storm he was feeling a lot better and to this day I am impressed with his ability to recover in such a short time from a night like that.

We never stopped for gas on these trips because he owned a gas station and the cars in those days didn't have all of the bells and whistles of today that reduce gas mileage.

However, when we stopped in Mt. Storm to switch drivers he bought me an ice cream cone at the general store, which by now I knew was a combination treat and bribe for "keeping my own counsel" as he called it.

Then on down the mountain to the roadhouse and the last business trip to Petersburg, that I went on, was over.

Chapter Nine

Upon arriving back at the roadhouse that time we found that Aunt Vera and grandma had some excitement of their own while we were in Petersburg. In fact when we pulled into the driveway the Sheriff was putting a tall blonde-haired guy, who was handcuffed and limping, and looked like he had been "drug through a knothole," into the back of his pick-up truck.

But the first thing that happened right after we left for Petersburg was that a dairy farmer by the name of Jess stopped in the roadhouse for a bite to eat. He stopped in often and had always flirted with Aunt Vera in a casual way.

He had a huge sheepdog named Chigger, that was bigger than Trooper, which he had trained to herd his cows in for milking. I remember wondering why he had a sheepdog to chase cows. "Unc' had asked Jess more than once not to bring Chigger into the roadhouse where Trooper was because he didn't want them to fight. Jess' reaction was that Chigger could handle himself and that he would probably kill Trooper. Since he was not too cooperative my uncle would instruct Trooper to go back into the kitchen when Jess brought Chigger in with him. It happened often enough so that when Chigger came in Trooper would get up from leaning against the counter and head towards the kitchen. Jess usually commented that he forgot to leave Chigger outside because he was "used to him being underfoot all the time!".

I think that Jess mistook Trooper's reaction for fear in the way he would head back to the kitchen in response to my uncle's order.

As usual Jess brought Chigger inside with him and since Trooper was already in the kitchen with Aunt Vera and grandma, Aunt Vera left him there and went out to the counter to see what Jess wanted to eat.

Jess was known to make liquor for his own consumption and it wasn't long until Aunt Vera realized that he had been consuming some before he arrived at the roadhouse and was in a very amorous mood. It was also obvious that he knew that my uncle wasn't home.

Aunt Vera knew how to deal with men who had too much to drink and could usually control them pretty well. She suggested that Jess have coffee in place of the beer he ordered with his sandwich but he had fed some nickels into the juke box and grabbed her as she turned to go back to the kitchen and received an elbow in the ribs. He grabbed her again and pulled her close, pinning her arms to her sides stating that he didn't come by just to eat and intended to find out if she was as good as she looked.

Aunt Vera raised her voice and called out to Trooper who came out of the kitchen and around the counter with a low growl. Jess spoke Chiggers name without any hesitation and the dog came to his feet from against the wall where he was laying and charged Trooper across the dance floor. Trooper saw Chigger a little too late because he was looking at Aunt Vera and Jess so that when Chigger, with his superior size plowed into Trooper he sent him rolling across the floor and up against the wall. Aunt Vera said that she thought the fight was over until Trooper sprang to his feet and met Chigger in a head on rush and Chigger again rolled Trooper across the floor and up against the wall.

Jess, who was still holding Aunt Vera, began to laugh and said that he had been told that Trooper was a dangerous dog and here he was getting his ass handed to him.

At that point the two dogs charged each other again only this time Trooper went in under Chigger as the larger dog attempted to repeat his previous moves and clamped on Chiggers rear paw, and then he rolled, and you could hear bone break. In a split second Trooper was up and had Chigger by the throat.

In that brief moment, Jess lost interest in Aunt Vera and rushed to the two dogs trying to get Trooper to let go of Chigger. Upon realizing that he could not separate them he pleaded with my aunt to call Trooper off, saying that the dog was his livelihood.

Aunt Vera could not get Trooper to let go and it took my grandmother who called his name in her soft, quiet voice to get him to release Chigger.

My mother had this picture taken because she thought the
pony looked like Socks.

My Dad.

Uncle Jamie - high school graduation.

Uncle Jamie - the early years.

My Mother and Uncle Jamie with his daughter-in-law in the middle.

Uncle Jamie and my mother in front of the roadhouse.

Trooper

Grandmother and Trooper

Saddle Mountain, Rt#50, between Mt. Storm and the turnoff to Keyser, West Virginia.

Without a word, Jess picked up Chigger, carried him out and put him in the bed of his truck. In a few minutes he was driving up the mountain towards Mt. Storm.

That should have been all of the excitement my aunt and grandmother had for one day but it was not to be.

The rest of the day was pretty quiet until mid-afternoon when a tall blonde-haired guy was dropped off in front of the roadhouse by a coal truck, which was on the way back to one of the mines in the area.

He strolled into the roadhouse and ordered a hamburger and beer from my aunt and listened to the jukebox for a while. Trooper came out from the kitchen to check him out and after being petted a little bit wandered back into the kitchen with my grandmother.

The guy, who introduced himself as Richard or Rich for short, asked my aunt when the Greyhound bus was due going east and she informed him that it would not be until the following morning about 10am. He replied that he had been working in one of the coalmines for the summer but was returning home to Winchester, Virginia because his parents were getting older and needed help with their business. He asked if the cabins were for rent just for one night and my aunt replied that they were.

During the rest of the afternoon and evening he casually strolled around the property even going off in the woods, up the hill behind the roadhouse for a while. He tried to get Trooper to go with him but Trooper didn't seem to be very interested.

When the man returned from the woods he laid down on the picnic table and stayed there for at least an hour and a half, which was just about, dusk when he came into the roadhouse for dinner.

Aunt Vera said that they had more than the usual number of people for dinner so that she didn't talk to him except he did ask if she wanted to sell the Dodge sedan parked in the back of the building and she replied that it was not for sale. For some reason she couldn't explain she added that he could talk to her husband anyway when he got home later that evening if he was serious about buying it. He asked if it was in running condition and she replied yes, that it was started up almost every day.

After he finished eating he sat at the table nursing a couple of beers until everyone else had left and my aunt was closing up for the night.

He then asked if he could bunk downstairs on the floor for the night until the bus arrived in the morning. My aunt told him that her husband would not allow it and that he was due to arrive home at any time.

He then asked if he could rent one of the cabins and pay her everything he owed after breakfast in the morning.

Aunt Vera said that she began to feel uneasy around the guy by that time and she suspected he did not have the money to pay his bill in the first place.

But she didn't want a confrontation at that time of night so she agreed, fully expecting not to be paid in the morning or any other time for that matter. Having helped many other drifters off and on she felt that this would just be one more.

She opened up the cabin closest to the roadhouse for him while Grandma and Trooper watched from the back door. Then she, my grandmother, and Trooper went upstairs to bed after she closed up the roadhouse.

Sometime before sunrise, Trooper woke my aunt with a low whine and growl. Once she was fully awake she could hear some soft scraping and tapping somewhere outside. Then she heard the soft muffled sound of breaking glass downstairs. At that, Trooper was out of the bedroom and down the stairs before Aunt Vera could stop him. Almost immediately she heard a loud curse, a short yelp of pain from Trooper, then a grunt and another curse just before a loud crash and cry of pain, and then a mans voice yelling and cursing above the noise of furniture crashing around and against the walls.

By this time, my grandmother was awake and was on the phone to the Sheriff and Aunt Vera was on her way downstairs with the 32 cal. pistol my uncle kept in the dresser drawer next to the bed. She said that she was very worried about Trooper because of the yelp she had heard.

When she reached the bottom of the stairs and switched on the lights she saw the blonde haired man by the name of Richard being dragged around the dance floor. Trooper had clamped his jaws around the mans leg between the ankle and the knee and had pulled him the the rest of the way through the window when the man had his leg over the sill to step inside the room. Tables and chairs were scattered about the room where Trooper had dragged him and there was quite a bit of blood on the floor from the mans head and Trooper was bleeding from his side where the man had stabbed him with a knife.

As soon as my aunt saw the knife she pointed the pistol at the man and told him to toss the knife away or she would shoot him. My grandmother came down to tell Aunt Vera that the Sheriff was on his way and she had to tell Trooper to let go of the mans leg. They were sure that he was no danger to them at this point because they knew his leg was seriously hurt. They didn't find out until later that it was broken just above the ankle.

Troopers wound was not serious, the veterinarian said that it did not hit anything vital when he stitched it up and that Trooper would be his old self in a very short time. He didn't seem to me to be any other self, then!

The law arrived soon after my grandmother had come downstairs and handcuffed the man and was putting him in his truck when my uncle and I drove into the driveway.

Aunt Vera told my uncle that it would be a very cool day in hell the next time he left her and his mother alone at the roadhouse, overnight, again!

I don't remember ever seeing Jess at the roadhouse after that but I did overhear my uncle say that almost losing his dog was fair punishment for his actions because he couldn't fault any man for wanting to get his hands on Vera. Whether that was his only punishment is anybody's guess because wanting to and doing was "over the line"!

I think that Richard thought that he had made a friend of Trooper, which was a big mistake. He also figured out that my uncle was not going to be home that night, which was fortunate for him because there is a big difference between a trip to the jailhouse and a trip to the morgue.

Chapter Ten

Most of the people my age whom I met during those summers in the mountains were friendly and easy to get along with. But there was one guy who lived up not far from the roadhouse who was a bully. He was 2 to 3 years older than I, about the same age as big "D", and well set up physically with a muscular build. He was obviously pretty strong because he prepped the field next to his house with a hand plow. That was pretty impressive as far as most of us were concerned. He didn't mess with big "D" or with most of the other guys when big "D" was around because he knew that he would have to fight and he wasn't too sure of his chances with him. I never saw big "D" pick a fight or run from one and he always looked out for us younger guys, usually with a smile that said we have things to do that are a whole lot more fun.

I can hardly remember the bully's name. I think it was Rod, short for Roderick. Rod didn't hesitate to push the rest of us guys around when big "D" wasn't there.

He had a mean streak and his idea of what was funny was when he could trick someone into a bad experience regardless of the negative consequences. In fact, he really got a kick out of tricking someone into being hurt or hurting themselves. When we had our mock battles at the wood shaving fort he didn't just throw cow pie at the other person; he would get them down and rub their face with it.

And, when big "D" would pull him off and ask him how he would like it, he would laugh and say he was just kidding around. Sometimes he would help the person up and go through the motions of wiping them off but we all knew that he didn't mean it.

My one on one experience with Rod was shortly after big "D" went with his dad on a trucking trip to, I think, Cleveland, Ohio.

Every Saturday night the church in Mt. Storm would show movies for anyone who wished to attend and pay 5 cents admission for those who could afford it.

Not long after big "D" left with his dad my uncle asked me if I would like to go to the movies in Mt. Storm with a group of kids who were going to ride up to Mt. Storm and back in one of the farmer's pickup trucks the following Saturday night.

Of course I wanted to go and didn't hesitate to climb in the back of the truck with the rest of the kids when they picked me up in front of the roadhouse.

I wasn't completely surprised to find that Rod was in the group but I couldn't help but feel disappointed and when he called out, "hey Britchy", I made the mistake of telling him that only my uncle called me that. Of course that was the wrong thing to say and the three mile trip up the mountain was not pleasant with him poking at me and calling me

"Britchy" every few minutes. Most of the other kids didn't join in because they all had been the brunt of Rod's attention. One or two would laugh when he would look at them because, I suspect, they didn't want him to start on them.

The farmer dropped us off in front of the church and told Rod where he would pick us up after the movies were over. I heard him mention a family name that indicated the house he was referring to which was not familiar to me since I was not familiar with all of the people who lived in the village. But since there were hardly more than a dozen houses along the road through the village I figured I could find it if necessary.

The movies were pretty good including "Felix The Kat", "Our Gang", and a couple of "Popeye The Sailor's," which were the usual at that time and we all enjoyed them even with Rod talking loud and often until one of the few adults there told him to shut up.

But by the time the movies were over he had picked up on the "Otay Panky" line from the "Our Gang" movie and was using it almost constantly while holding one of his hands up with his fingers forming the okay sign.

However, when I got outside of the church none of the guys, including Rod, were there and most of the people were leaving in cars and trucks as well as beginning to walk home. In a short amount of time I was by my self outside the church, in the dark, and the only lights I could see were in the back of the general store and a few porch lights at houses along the road.

Not knowing which house we would be picked up at I began to walk in the direction of the roadhouse because all of the houses were situated on both sides of the road in that direction.

It didn't take me very long to figure out that Rod was playing one of his little games because I would hear him call out "Otay Panky-Britchie" every now and then, or "Otay Britchie-Panky" and when I would approach a house I would catch glimpses of shadows or movements of people running away from the house into the darkness and hear some laughing along with the "Otay" business.

By the time I reached the next to the last house just before the road began to pitch down the mountain towards the roadhouse I could see a group of people sitting in the light on the porch and turned into the gravel driveway. About halfway to the porch I could see Rod put his hand on the railing of the porch and vault over onto the grass and he yelled out, "Otay Britchie, you found us, now what are ya goin' to do now that big "D" isn't around to take up fer ya?"

I said that I wasn't going to do anything and didn't know what he was talking about, and I just wanted my ride back to my uncle's. Rod laughed and said that he hadn't decided whether he was going to let me ride back with them or make me walk. I guess I didn't realize how mad I was getting at that point when I told him I didn't care whether I rode or walked and was sick and tired of him and his silly games.

By this time all of the others were standing around listening and watching to see what was going to happen when Rod pushed me and asked what I was going to do about it. I said that I had told him that I wasn't going to do anything when he pushed me again. I turned to walk away when he pushed me on the back of my head.

That's when I lost control and turned back towards him. I pushed his hand away from the back of my head with my right hand and sunk my left fist into his stomach as hard as I could. As soon as I hit him I remember thinking I had done a dumb thing and had better keep swinging for as long as I could. Expecting him to be doubled over from the punch in the stomach I swung my right fist as hard as I could where I thought his face should be and missed him completely. My feet went out from under me in the gravel driveway and I landed hard, flat on my back, which knocked the wind out of me. Laying on the ground, trying to get my breath back, I kept expecting to be hit or kicked but nothing happened and when I did start breathing again and got to my feet I could see Rod laying on the ground at the foot of a large tree holding his stomach. He was groaning and had vomited all over himself. It seemed that when I hit him in the stomach he didn't just bend over, but was driven back at the same time so when I swung again he wasn't there.

I walked over to where he was laying and he looked up at me and rasped out, "What did ya do that fer?" The only thing I could think to say was, "You asked for it," and he did!

No one said a word as I walked out of the driveway and on my way to a three-mile walk down the mountain to the roadhouse. That walk was scary with no light and animal noises sounding out of the woods. I kept thinking that it would be my luck to run into a bobcat without Trooper along.

Halfway down the mountain the pick up truck pulled along side with everyone in it and the farmer said for me to get in but I was still mad and refused. I felt that he should have kept Rod in line so that none of it would have happened.

The thing that I learned from that incident that helped me out more times than I am proud to admit is that no matter how big and strong they are, they can't fight if they can't breathe!

Chapter Eleven

The following morning my uncle got me out of bed early, and told me to get dressed because we were going to Keyser which is about 25 miles up, over, and down the seven mile run past the valley where Nancy Hanks, who was Abe Lincoln's mother, was born. Keyser was a railhead at the time with a large switching yard. We had some relatives who I can't remember much about except the father was some kind of railroad hero. It seems he was injured while on duty but managed to switch tracks in time to avert a train crash.

Anyway, it turned out to be a fun trip. "Unc" bought me lunch at a nice diner, took me to the movies and introduced me to the game of pool. After we shot a few games of pool he took me into a men's clothing store and bought me a pair of long dress pants, shoes, a shirt and tie, and a sport coat. He said I was getting big enough to dress, as he put it," to the nines", when I went out "sportin". Years later, my sister told me that my mother was very upset about him buying me the clothes because she felt cheated. I of course had overalls and khakis that I wore to bang around in and go to school in but he bought me my first pair of long dress pants!

After we left the clothing store we went to a

nice restaurant on Main Street before we headed back up the mountain and "Unc" flirted with the pretty waitress while we ate dinner. At one point he leaned over to me and said,"Wouldn't you like to bite her in the ass and let her drag you all over town?" Although I was past puberty and thought about girls, and was a little embarassed, I still got a feeling of comaraderie with him and never forgot how he treated me that day. Even after my aunt told me that the trip was his way of showing how proud he was of me for "licking that big bully" the night before in Mt. Storm. I don't know how they found out about it although I am sure somebody told them.

    I only saw Rod a few times after our "go round" and he never mentioned it when I did. Although he was civil he wasn't friendly and his father was cool towards me when he came into the roadhouse on business. It didn't bother my uncle one bit, he acted as if everything was just the same, in fact he seemed to over do it a bit.

    I learned something else from that experience. I learned that people who witnessed your actions with that kind of outcome see you differently than they did before. You didn't feel any different but they are different towards you. In fact, the other guy's friends usually don't see him start it and your friends see you more competent than you really are. Anyway, the happy-go-lucky relationship with the rest of the guys was never quite the same. My uncle said that people tended to believe what was advantageous to them or what they wanted to whether it was true or not. I found that to be profound and witnessed it many times over the years.

When big "D" heard about it he grabbed me around the waist and picked me up and danced around whooping and laughing.

He told me that the only thing he didn't like about it, was that he missed it!

I learned something else about my uncle that summer that I never forgot.

A few days after the trip to Keyser my uncle asked me if I would like to go with the Amoco Truck driver when he delivered gas to a couple of small mining towns back in the mountains off from the main highway.

The truck would deliver to the roadhouse and then make a delivery run up to these two towns and then return past the roadhouse on the way back to the gas depot.

That sounded like a fun trip because it was mostly wild country and I was sure I would see a lot of animal life on the way up and back.

The ride to the first town was interesting and the ride overall was a little scary because it was a big truck on small, almost single lane country roads with steep cliffs falling away down into the valley. Jiggs, the truck driver, seemed like a nice guy but didn't have too much to say and I figured that he was concentrating on the road.

We pulled into the first town and into the one

gas station which was also a repair garage and machine shop and Jiggs got out and hooked his hose up to the in-ground tank, and opened up the fill valve. I helped as much as I could and when we were through Jiggs asked me if I wanted a soda pop and I said sure and thanked him when he handed it to me.

More than a few people had gradually showed up and were standing around outside the station when a boy about my age walked into the driveway and headed towards the building office. As he passed by me he reached out with his elbow and knocked my soda out of my hand.

He stopped and told me to stay out of his way. When I didn't answer and reached down to pick up the soda bottle he kicked it away from me and told me again to stay out of his way. I think I mumbled something about not thinking that I was in his way when he hit me in the mouth which stumbled me back into the one gas pump. No one there moved to interfere, including Jiggs, which told me that I was on my own with this kid.

I pushed myself off of the gas pump with tears in my eyes, crouched a little and put my guard up while he strutted back and forth calling me names and telling me what he was going to do to me. He was well built and muscular and maybe just a little bit bigger than me, and I was scared and mad at the same time.

We started to circle one another and after a few seconds when neither one of us made a real move towards the other a man in the crowd yelled, "Git it over with boy!"

At that he lowered his head and charged me. Somehow I dodged him and as he stumbled by I grabbed him from behind around the throat with my forearm across his Adam's apple, grabbed my wrist with my other hand and started to squeeze as hard as I could. He tried to tear himself loose, hit me back over his shoulder, trip me, and reach around for my groin before we both fell to the ground. When we landed on the ground I locked both of my legs around the lower part of his body, arched my back and continued to squeeze him across the throat as hard as I could.

Sometime during all of this I thought I heard Jiggs yell "They'll be none of that!".

All at once the kid went limp and somehow I knew to let go. We both laid there for a while. He started to breath in gulps after a time and I got up and leaned against the gas truck. He got to his knees after a little while, but still gasping for air. He didn't stay on his knees very long when he got to his feet still shaking and breathing hard. At this point I heard the same voice as before yell out "Wait 'till I get you home boy!" When I looked towards the voice that spoke I could see Jiggs holding a man from behind in a bearhug. Jiggs was a pretty big man and he was holding the other man with very little effort. When I looked back at the kid, I was surprised to see him approaching me with his fists up. This time he was moving slow and deliberate. All I could think of was, that I wanted to get out of there but I knew that there was only one way to do that.

He didn't look as sure of himself as before and still showed difficulty in breathing so wanting to get it over with I charged him with fists up. This time we met head on with no strategy, both of us throwing fists as hard and as fast as we could and even though he was winded and tired he stood toe to toe with me until he went down backwards. I was just about through myself when he struggled back up and went down again with a fist to the side of the head, this time to stay and I couldn't help feeling some satisfaction to see that he was crying.

Everyone there was talking to each other while Jiggs handed me a cold, wet cloth and put me in the cab of the truck. He had shut down the filling operation sometime before the fight so he went in to the office to get the papers signed and stopped on the way out to speak to two men before getting back into the truck. As he pulled the truck out on the road in the direction of the next town I could see most of the people who had been at the station walking towards the houses built on the side of the hill down from the gas station. And I caught a glimpse of the boy's father dragging him by the arm along the road in the same direction. I couldn't help feeling sorry for him at that time.

Jiggs didn't say a word while we drove to the next town, filled up the in-ground tank of the one pump gas station, and headed back towards my uncle's roadhouse. It was all right with me because I was busy tending to my cuts and bruises. I had a cut and swollen lip, two loose teeth, my left eye was almost swollen shut, and my nose didn't stop bleeding until just before we left the second town. I sure didn't feel like the winner!

A little while after we pulled out of the second town Jiggs said, "Listen kid, I'm sorry about that back there. You should know by now that it was a set-up. But that was one of the best scraps I ever saw bar none, and that was the first lickin' that kid ever took. His old man was sure surprised when you put him in that throat lock and I had to keep him from steppin' in."

When Jiggs dropped me off at the roadhouse he shook my hand as if I was a grown man and I clenched my teeth because both hands were swollen. He looked at my uncle and said, "Thats a helluva kid there Jim!" Aunt Vera saw me, gave my uncle a dirty look, and got me upstairs before my grandmother could see me.

I never knew how much money my uncle won on that fight and it figures that Jiggs got a piece of the action given the way things went.

I was always glad that I didn't have to find out what the reaction would have been if I had lost!

You know, somehow I never felt any resentment towards my uncle for that.

I figure it's because, like the rest of the family, I had already accepted him as he was and besides, my dad always said to look at all of life's experiences as a learning situation.

Well, that was some learning situation because, thinking about it, if that boy's father hadn't goaded him into charging me at first, and I would have had to fight him fresh, toe to toe, I would have had my ass handed to me as they used to say.

Chapter Twelve

I think I got a pretty well rounded practical education during the summers I spent in the mountains at my uncle's roadhouse.

Besides everything I have described so far I also picked plums for five cents an hour and helped slaughter a cow the old fashioned way where the cow was shot between the eyes out in the pasture before the throat was cut and hung from a tree for drainage, skinning, and dissection. I worked for a short while in a lumber camp where I was taught to work the opposite end of a cross cut saw for hours at a time without "riding" it which was interfering with your partner's pull by pushing it back at him. That was a big no-no!

One time I spent one week out of the summer at one of my uncle's former partner's farm where they raised ponies to work in the mines near-by. I was allowed to feed them and helped herd them to a different pasture once. I also could ride any one I wanted to as long as I could catch and stay on them. I had a pretty close call when I walked up on the wrong side of a paint that was blind in one eye while we were still in a stall inside the barn. It was a good thing that the sides of the stall were rickety and flimsy because when he began to kick and attempt to turn away from me he hipped me through them and out into the barn. Needless to say I went home to my uncle's with a lot of bruises in just one week! But the times I had with the ponies that week were worth most of them!

I remember that the man and his wife didn't have any kids and the lady spoiled me with cookies and cakes the whole week, and cried when I left. I only knew them as Mr. and Mrs. Claude.

My uncle also got me a job one summer for about a month in one of the mines close by. My job was to do anything I was told to do without question as my uncle put it. I made 50 cents a day and at the end of the week I thought I was rich!

In addition to the miscellaneous tasks I had to do, I harnessed, unharnessed, and cared for the ponies that pulled the coal carts in and out of the mines, before and after the work day. They weren't "housebroke" so I also cleaned up after them during the day so the men wouldn't step in it when they went in and out of the mines. The work started before sunrise six days a week and the whistle didn't blow until just before dusk. At 50 cents a day I made less by the hour than picking plums but it taught me how to give a decent days work, and keep my mouth shut!

I saw more than one man, who had been fired for bitching and moaning too much, going down the road, "talking to himself," as they called it. My dad always said that if you didn't like the way things went on a job to keep your mouth shut until you found a different one. Sometimes I found that the next one was a better one!

Times sure have changed!

But life was real, we didn't have mans laws interpreted in a way that contradicts the laws of nature, dictates how one must think, live, work, play and do business. If there were such laws they would have been more impossible to enforce than they are now. Nor did we have self-proclaimed experts with no personal experience in the subject offering cop-out excuses for your unacceptable behavior.

You knew that government couldn't protect you from all dangers and disappointments and it was your responsibility to deal with your problems. If you couldn't resolve them, you protected yourself as best you could and got on with the business of living and surviving. There wasn't much time for feeling sorry for yourself when most of your time was spent trying to survive.

I can't remember seeing anyone arrested for defending themselves during my summers in the mountains. When the law showed up which was usually after most of the damage was done, they asked questions, sorted out who the culprit was and arrested only if a warrant was sworn by a creditable person, with standing, backed up by appropriate witnesses. It wasn't a perfect system but I don't see any significant improvement today that justifies the reduction in allowable judgment by law enforcement people at the location, and I don't see where the inconsistencies of law enforcement in the field have been reduced. I believe that we definitely have a social, juvenile-based problem in this country, but I also believe that the evidence of failed efforts have been ignored for many years!

But I digress because that last summer was not a happy time.

Trooper had died the previous winter. My Aunt Vera had taken him with her when she visited a sick woman friend who could not do her own grocery and medicine shopping. She had left the passenger window partly down so that he would have some air when she got out of the car. However she did not know that the women had been feeding a stray dog and it attacked my aunt when she opened the gate to the yard. Trooper went out through the window of the car and killed the dog but when he went through the window, the glass broke and slit his stomach open. My aunt didn't realize what had happened right away because she thought that all of the blood was from the dog fight.

I was told that when she did she drove Trooper straight to the vet in Mt. Storm who operated on Trooper without permission and he died on the operating table. My aunt told me that the first thing she did was go home and hide my uncle's guns and then call the Sheriff to come and restrain him from going up to the vets office when he was told.

Besides that, big "D"'s family moved because they did not own the land they farmed and the father accepted a job as a full time truck driver with a company based in Keyser. I was told that "Big D" went into the army soon after that as World War ll was under way. I also heard that Rod was in one of the military branches but in all honesty I didn't miss him too much. I never heard anymore about either one of them and don't know whether they survived the war or not. I often wondered whether big "D"'s happy-go-lucky outlook was good to him. I sure did hope so!

I hoped that Rod made it through too because our personal difficulties became insignificant compared to what he would face in the war, and I felt he needed all of the good wishes he could get.

Mr. Ty passed away that summer and the family sold the property and moved away. I don't know what happened to Socks. He probably went with the property or was sold separately even though Mr. Ty promised me he was mine. My uncle said that unless Mr. Ty left Socks to me in his will his family did not have to keep his promise.

I didn't understand that at the time but I found out later that Mr. Ty didn't leave a will probably because the property went to the family by law anyway and he must have thought that they would keep his promise for him. Or he just was too sick to think about his promise which was something I could understand. I never saw Socks again anyway and as you can see, the mountain wasn't the same! I wouldn't have been able to keep him anyway living in the city during the winter!

That was my last summer on the mountain. The next year I hitch hiked to Ocean City, Md. and got a lifeguard job on the beach for the summer. Soon after the summer was over and I had returned home to Washington DC, my mother strongly suggested I join the navy probably because of the people I was hanging out with and the type of activity I was getting involved in, plus the fact that I wasn't doing that well in school. I remember pointing out to my mother that some people were still shooting at each other at the time but she said that she was not worried about me and it looked like it all would be over soon. Besides, my mother stressed the benefits of the G.I. Bill and that I could pick up where I left off on my education when I got out.

My mother passed away while I was in the navy and the next time I would see my uncle would be in Clarksburg at her funeral.

By that time he had sold the Roadhouse and moved back to Clarksburg where he had bought a neighborhood grocery store. It was the kind that we call a "Mom and Pop" operation today. The store was on the first floor and the living quarters were on the second floor accessed by stairs in the back of the building.

I was in the Chelsea Naval Hospital outside of Boston, Massachusetts with a leg infection when I got word about my mother being sick and was in a fog because she passed on rather quickly since she did not seek medical help when she should have. So the funeral was pretty hazy to me except I do remember that my dad and I ended up at the grocery store afterwards to visit before we drove back to DC.

Evidently my uncle recognized my state of mind because he suggested I stay and talk when my dad expressed interest in visiting some other relatives before returning to DC. After my dad left, my uncle got a couple of beers out of the ice box and told me to get two orange crates from in back of the store to sit on. We took the crates and beers out in front of the store on the sidewalk and after a time he began to tell me about his younger days when he and his partners were in the liquor business in a matter-of-fact tone of voice.

For some reason, this elderly man with a white apron, bow tie, and a dress Stetson hat on, with the brim turned up in the front and the back like a traditional news reporter, slightly overweight, beer in one hand and a cigarette in the other, began telling me the story of his youth.

Beginning with, "I made a lot of money in my time, Britchy. Had a lot of fun and made a lot of mistakes...... spent a lot of money on good times and bad, mostly bad when my luck ran out! Thats when the "Feds" stepped in and sent me to the state pen in Elkins for what they called a violation of federal prohibition laws. Hell, most people felt that it wasn't any of their damn business what we drank or where we got it from, and if they got away with that there would be no end to what they stuck their noses into.

But Elkins wasn't so bad. I knew most of the boys up there and they treated me pretty good. I was able to make pocket money in the poker games we had and I even made a few Saturday night party trips outside with the night boss in the two years I was there. Sometimes I would be nursing a pretty good hangover when your mom and some of the family came to visit on Sunday afternoons. But the gist of what I am telling you is that I had plenty of money when I was arrested and after the fines, payoffs, and the attorneys got through with me, I was just about tap city. If it wasn't for Claude and Shorty, I would have been in bad shape money-wise when I got out. Yet it was only right for them to "pony-up" because I took the rap!"

Chapter Thirteen

"We were just a bunch of young guys," my uncle continued, "who thought the world was our oyster. We all had met and got to know each other through the 'let it all hang out party' years following World War I. Historians refer to the time as 'The Roaring Twenties'.

Every night was party night and Claude, Shorty, Whitey and me would meet usually, at the pool hall on Pike Street, with or without dates, for a night of gambling, drinking, and dancing, and whatever if the ladies showed up.

We would bring our own personal brew of beer or liquor when we got together and kid each other about whose was the best until one night we decided to pool our recipes and see what we came up with. After a few tries we were surprised to come up with a mix that was well received amongst the general population. A whole lot of people made their own in those days because the parents were originally from someplace else where they made their own and brought that practice with them. Practically all of the 'Krauts' made a brew of some kind, mostly beer, in the bathtub. The 'Shanty Irish' would drink anything and they were usually a lot of trouble if you hung around too long with 'em. But a lot of gin was made in the bathtubs, that's how the name 'bathtub gin' got started. The street joke the kids sang was 'slop up that gin when it gets to yer chin, ya could all drown if you don't slurp it down'.

The 'Eye-ties' kept to themselves mostly but got a little pushy after the business began to grow because they realized how much money we were making. We stayed out of 'Eye-tie' town unless we had business there, but we had to go over there a few times during the busy years when they made it necessary.

When we first got into the business I was working at the Chicago Dairy, on the corner of Second and Main, as a baker, doughnuts were my specialty but I also baked cakes and pies. Shorty's dad owned the pool hall and saloon that we hung out in. We drank, and played cards and dice on the second floor after hours. A distant cousin of your dad's was a police officer so we were left alone pretty much. He made chief in later years. Claude's dad had passed on and left him a pretty good chunk of land in the mountains between the 'seven mile run' and Mt. Storm.

Whitey was in sales. I couldn't keep track of everything he sold but he usually had or could get whatever you wanted whenever you wanted it for a price and he wasn't choosey about what he sold or who he sold it to!

At first we all just took orders and delivered the stuff separately but got together once a week to settle up with each other so that no one lost out. However

, soon we noticed that we weren't stocking up enough because we would have to take off from selling and delivering to cook up stock. We had set up a small still on Claude's property at first but it soon became obvious that it was too small and we had to add a second one as well as leave Claude there to run the stills almost full time. Claude also had a couple of pro football players from the Redskins helping him out during the off season. They would pick up the slack wherever we needed them as we got busier.

That forced us into taking a hard look at our operation and making some adjustments. The result was a pretty sweet, and I might add, slick way of doing business. Business was still good and continued to grow even when the economy slowed. Seemed like people handled hard times with a good time!

We set up a half a dozen stills in a blind draw, which was a good distance from the highway, in the most remote part of Claude's property. The entrance to the draw was fairly narrow so we stretched a clothes line from one side to the other with two German shepherd dogs connected to the line so they could roam the entrance without getting tangled up with each other. Those two dogs let Claude know when anyone was coming while he was tending the stills. In fact one of the dogs jumped one of the football players when he failed to let Claude know that he was coming. Claude broke it up before one of them hurt the other. Claude said that it looked like it was 'even-steven' when he got there!

I set up a coffee and doughnut shop in Clarksburg, just off Main Street, on Second Street. We had a room in the back for those who wanted something a little stronger than coffee. Even though a lot of our customers came from all over and represented all areas of influence, it was still pretty bold to have our shop so close to city hall which was on Main Street.

Shorty transported the stuff from the farm to the shop and made deliveries to special customers throughout the county and eventually the state. His dad was one of our best customers who served our stuff to the pool players in his place.

Whitey, handled sales and public relations and kind of took on security as it became necessary. Whitey could smell a rat before it showed it's tail. He handled all negotiations with customers and competitors. He was one of the most deceptive men I ever knew with a pleasant manner and pleasant looks that could go sour in a split second when he was confronted with an unreasonable attitude. Most of the people we dealt with were 'up front kinda guys' and Whitey would be more than cooperative in order to get an understanding with the shirt on his back as part of the deal if necessary. But when he ran into a guy who wanted the whole pie with a take it or leave it attitude he became one mean son of a bitch. More than one guy ended up with no pie at all and a 'some kinda hurtin' to boot'. Whitey and your dad were two guys that I would not want to take on unless I had no other choice.

Whitey was the reason our business grew as quickly as it did. Of course, the stuff we made was good but Whitey was the guy who got out and sold it to everyone he could think of. The doughnut shop was so popular it was very seldom empty when it was open. It was so popular that the 'Feds' knew where to go when they came to call!

Don't get me wrong, we weren't anything like the big city boys, we were just a few local guys making a good living doing what we liked to do.

But there were a few times we had to protect our interests because if you don't people begin to think they can walk on you!

I remember one time the 'Eye-ties' latched on to some of our stuff that Shorty had stored in a garage up in Fairmont. How they knew it was there is anybody's guess but we knew they had it because the owner saw them break the lock and haul it off in broad daylight. There was more than one reason why he didn't bother to call the cops!

They always had a big dance every Saturday night in 'Eye-tie' town so we decided to stop in and have a chat with the guys who we were pretty sure had our stuff. Shorty, Whitey and me with a few friends stopped in and asked them for a talk outside. We all went outside in the parking area and the long and the short of it was, we got our liquor back!

There were other situations over time where we had to let people know we wouldn't roll over when they tried to move in! Most of them were easily handled but things got serious when some boys from Pittsburgh showed up!

Chapter Fourteen

One day, Whitey got in touch with me, Shorty and Claude, and said we needed to have a talk. We met the following night at the pool hall where Whitey informed us that a guy from Pittsburgh had approached him at the high school football game the past Friday afternoon. The guy had told Whitey that he wanted to help us expand our business and work out an arrangement. He said that his people heard that we were the ones to talk to about supplying quality stuff to a connection in Pittsburgh. He indicated that his people were unable to get enough to take care of their customers and were open for a deal with a supplier and would pay top dollar for all we could deliver. Whitey said that the guy and one of his partners wanted to meet with the four of us to discuss the details.

Claude didn't like that idea at all and flatly refused to meet with anyone outside our group. He felt that we would not only expose all of the members of our group to strangers from out of town but also open ourselves up to outside control. Shorty was all for it but felt that Whitey was our front man and should handle the deal the same as always. I didn't feel one way or the other at the time except ,as always I liked the idea of increasing our take.

Whitey, Shorty and I decided, over Claude's objection, that Whitey would meet with these two guys and report back to us with their offer.

We didn't hear from Whitey for over two weeks, didn't know where he was, and were beginning to get worried when he called Shorty and told him that he was in Pittsburgh getting wined and dined, 'laid and waylaid' with the guys that wanted to do business with us. He said that he should be back within a week and would let us know what was up when he did.

When Whitey got back from Pittsburgh we all met at the pool hall where he told us all about his trip and how he had 'painted the town red' with the guys he went to deal with. From what he could tell, they were the main connection with five locations operating seven nights a week. They were well protected with an understanding with the cops and not just the guys in the street. They wanted all we could deliver with a shipment at least once a week and 'cash on the barrel head,' which meant cash on delivery. Whitey said as soon as we gave them the word that we were in, he would get with them to work out the details of communications and delivery location, or locations.

Claude stated that he was still against doing business with them but since he was out voted he felt it would not be wise to deliver to more than one location. He stated that any more than one location after the trip up there would put too much exposure on Shorty. He also felt that Whitey may be getting too cozy with the guys from Pittsburgh and wouldn't be able to handle any disagreements or spot problems in time to head them off.

Although Claude didn't like the deal he went along with the three of us and we worked out the details over a couple of weeks. Our first delivery went as smooth as silk and Shorty came back with more cash money than any of us had seen since we got into the business. In fact it became obvious to us that Shorty should not make the run by himself, especially the return trip with that kinda' cash! After that we took turns going with Shorty and helping out with the driving.

Everything was going along great! Between the deliveries and the local trade we were taking in a lot of dough.

I guess the boys in 'Pitt' figured that once we got a taste of the rewards of the deal we would be hooked because it wasn't long before they began to relax on payment and wanted us to distribute the stuff at the various locations they operated. Shorty, of course, told them that a deal was a deal and refused to deliver to more than one location and demanded payment as agreed upon.

It was all in the talking stage until Shorty came back from a trip with no cash, no liquor, and roughed up pretty good!

Whitey blew his top. The three of us had to physically hold him down until he cooled off. He was ready to go up to 'Pitt' and take them all on. He swore he was going to personally 'stomp a mudhole in the one guy's ass'.

Well, we discontinued deliveries and didn't hear from 'Pitt' right away. But after about a week and a half Whitey got a call from them requesting that he come up for a talk. He was ready to go but the three of us out voted him and said they would have to come to us after what they had done to Shorty.

They agreed and we set the meeting up for the following Friday night at the pool hall.

Although at previous meetings they had sent two guys max, this time there were four of them which was not too hard to understand given the circumstances of the last few weeks. The guy that Whitey had been dealing with from the start was one of them and was still doing most of the talking if not all of it. He started off by telling us that the guys that did Shorty were severely disciplined. They had acted on their own and were no longer with the company. He stated that they were still interested in doing business with us under the terms of the original agreement and assured us that nothing like the incident with Shorty would happen again. He added that they were not just interested, but needed our product!

One of the guys had picked up a pool cue and was taking shots on one of the tables. He kept interrupting with cracks like, 'What are we pussy footin' around with these lightweights for? Tell 'em what to do and lets get back to Pitt'. The first guy finally hesitated, rolled his eyes at this guy and said, 'Not now, lets get this resolved'.

At one point Whitey asked where the guys were that did Shorty and the guy shooting pool said that he didn't want to know or go there because he might get some of what Shorty got! Whitey stood up and took a step towards the guy when we all stood up and Claude and Shorty stepped in front of Whitey.

The first guy said, 'Hey, wait a minute we don't need this at all, we need to settle our business, not do something stupid.'

I told the guy that we would talk it over and let him know in a few days. Meanwhile he and his friends should leave and give us all a chance to cool off. Whitey and the wiseguy kept eyeballin' each other while they all went down the steps and out the door. It was a very tense situation because we all knew that Whitey did not forget!

We all would have been a lot better off if we had of forgot all about doing business with them at that point but we had gotten used to that kind of money rolling in and didn't want to give it up. We started the deliveries again the following week with one of the footballers going along with Shorty to help with the driving, and whatever!

We didn't have any more problems with the boys from 'Pitt' and everything was just peachy when they asked us all up to 'Pitt' for a 'shindig,' to show their appreciation for our cooperation and business arrangement.

They promised a real 'blowout' with all of the people they did business with so every connection in the area would be there. They said that they did it at least once a year and it really paid off for everybody to get together and get to know one another.

Claude flat out refused to go, Shorty said he wouldn't go unless both Whitey and I went. Whitey and I decided to go because we felt that if we didn't it would make a bad situation worse and besides we were interested in seeing how things went.

We should never have gone because that turned out to be the beginning of a turn of bad luck. For one thing, I was getting mixed signals from Whitey. He acted as if nothing had ever happened between us and the 'Pitt' crowd. He kept saying that he was looking forward to that night and knew that we were going to have a great time. He even confided that maybe Shorty brought it on himself and we should do what we could to smooth things over. That was the first, and only, face to face discussion that Whitey and I ever had when I told him that I didn't want to hear that kinda' talk. We looked at each other for a while and then Whitey laughed and said he was just considering all of the possibles. Still, I had an uneasy feeling up to and including the night we drove up to 'Pitt'.

The affair was held at one of their locations in the suburbs. We felt that it was probably the biggest one they had because a pile of people were there. Every one looked like they wore their best 'bib and tucker' and there were some kinda' 'snappy lookin'' broads moving around serving drinks and being real friendly.

We were greeted by the main guy we had set up our business deal with who had one of the ladies show us to our table. Some other gals joined us in a very short while and we were having a real good time when I noticed that Whitey was missing. Shorty noticed me looking around and said that Whitey had gone to the men's room to talk to a guy he knew that went in there.

That didn't register right away but when it did I was half way to the men's room when I heard the shot and commotion that followed. Shorty was right behind me when we pushed the door open and found Whitey leaning up against the wall with a bloody towel bar in his hand. When he saw us he pointed to one of the two guys laying on the floor and said, 'that son-of-a-bitch tried to shoot me and that other son-of-a-bitch tried to brain me with this towel bar'. He had a pretty good bloody lump on the side of his head but was still in control of himself. Shorty picked up the pistol that was laying on the floor and stuck it in his coat pocket at about the time that the main guy pushed his way through the crowd that had gathered at the door to the room.

The guy that Whitey had pointed to was the guy that had threatened us at the last meeting. I had never seen the other guy before that night.

It turned out that Whitey had braced the guy

about who roughed up Shorty and the guy took a swing at him which was not a smart thing to do. Whitey flattened him and when he tried to pull a gun Whitey kicked it out of his hand as it went off. The guy that was with him caught Whitey with a glancing blow with the towel bar that he had pulled off the wall. Whitey took it away from him and proceeded to put both of them out of commission.

Chapter Fifteen

Needless to say, we left right after that. We didn't have to fight our way out but things were pretty tense although the main guy assured us that it wouldn't go any further and that we needed to continue with our deliveries. On the way back to Clarksburg Whitey admitted that he couldn't let that guy go on thinking that he had us 'buffaloed' but he didn't expect the reaction he got when he braced the guy. Whitey and I both felt a little better when Shorty said that the second guy was one of the bunch that roughed him up. At least one of them got some payback!

Both footballers wanted to go with Shorty on deliveries after that when they heard what happened. On of them said that he would ask the coach to give Whitey a crack at defensive lineman if you were allowed to take a towel bar on the field. Anyway, the deliveries stayed on schedule. Whether the two footballers headed off any problems we couldn't tell because the situation stayed the same even after they had to report back for the beginning of the football season.

I met with the head guy from 'Pitt', just me and him, in a diner just over the West Virginia line in Uniontown, Pa. It is a little bit more than half way between here and 'Pitt'. He said that the guys that

Whitey had the go-round with were not in solid with his group because they did do things on their own that put his people in a bad light, like the Shorty incident. He advised that we look out for the guy that pulled a gun on Whitey and I assured him that we would do that little thing. He seemed like a pretty right guy but I knew that he could not guarantee anything any more than I could. We promised to stay in touch because we both knew that we had a good deal going. I stayed the night with one of your dad's cousins and drove home the next day.

I got into Clarksburg about midday and went straight to the shop. Claude and Whitey were waiting to tell me that Shorty was sick and would not be able to make the delivery the next night. Since the footballers were in season it would be up to us to work it out. Claude reminded us that he was not for this deal in the first place so we could just forget about him making any deliveries. He would tend the stills but that was his end of the bargain and that was it! Whitey said, 'okay, okay, I will see if I can get one other guy if Jim can't get his brother Lee to help us out.' I reminded Whitey that my brother Lee was married to a woman who 'lived at the foot of the cross', and Lee couldn't take a leak without logging in and logging out!

Whitey said that he thought he knew a guy who might want to make a few bucks on the side but Claude didn't like the idea of bringing any one else in , even for one night. Whitey said that since Claude felt that way he would make the run by himself since Shorty had made it many times by himself. I didn't like that idea for obvious reasons and said that Claude would have to cover the home front and I would go with Whitey.

Whitey and I left early the next morning for the farm to load up the truck and then head on up to 'Pitt'. We pulled into the drop off about dinner time, had something to eat, and then unloaded. After we finished unloading we were told that we would have to go to another location to get our dough. I pointed out that it was not part of the deal and that we were to be paid at the delivery point. The guy made a big thing out of only doing as he was told. I wanted to talk to the main guy but I was told that he was not in touch at the time.

I didn't like it one bit and wanted to get on back to Clarksburg where we could take time to get in touch with the main guy and get things squared away. Whitey wasn't leaving 'Pitt' until he got our money! He wasn't easy to deal with when he made up his mind so we ended up following directions to the pick up location where we meet up with, 'guess who?'

Talk about bad luck! We pull into the parking lot, flash our lights, and two guys come out to meet us and one of them is the guy that Whitey had trouble with. We get out of the car and I know that Whitey is thinking the same thing I am because he puts his right hand in his coat pocket. I couldn't tell whether he had a gun or not but I had never known Whitey to carry one.

The surprising part was that the guy walked up to me and handed me an envelope and said, 'You can count it if you want to but it's all there'. With that he turned and walked back to the building . The second guy turned to Whitey and asked, 'Are you the one called Whitey?' and Whitey said, 'Yeah!'. The guy said, 'The next time I see you I'm gonna' beat you like a dirty rug'. As he walked away, Whitey said, 'Don't be late, and bring your lunch because your goin' to be there awhile!'

As I drove out of the parking lot Whitey wondered out loud about what that was all about and I said I had no idea.

It was on the steep grade outside of Uniontown that the car pulled alongside of us, as if to pass, and forced us off of the road down into a ravine where, after rolling, our truck ended up on my side against a bank of sheer rock. How I walked away from that one I will never know. I remember holding on to the wheel as hard as I could which maybe kept me from bouncing around in the cab. Whitey didn't make it! I crawled out on the hood through the broken windshield, stumbled around, and when I opened the door on the other side, Whitey fell out in my arms. Besides being cut up pretty bad, his neck was broken!

I was banged up pretty good and sore all over for a while but nothing permanent.

Shorty was all for going to 'Pitt' and settling up right away. It was all Claude and I could do to keep him from going. Along with Claude looking like he wanted to say that he told us so I argued that I wanted to talk to the main guy before we did anything. We finally agreed. I would get in touch with him and see what he had to say before anybody did anything.

I didn't have to get in touch with him, he called me first. Said he just heard what happened and wanted to talk. He was coming to Clarksburg, alone, to show good faith, because he trusted me to use good sense. I told him to make sure he did come alone and I would stand for his safety.

He showed up almost on the button of the time we agreed to and came directly to the doughnut shop where we went in to the back room to talk. Claude still wanted no part of him or his group and I did not feel that I could trust Shorty to hold his temper and listen to what he had to say.

He, of course denied knowing anything about the accident and I believed him when he told me that he did know that the two guys that paid us the money were the ones who did do it. They had set the whole thing up with the guy at the first location. He had the money to pay us but was told that it was to be a joke on us. He said that the wiseguy really had it in for Whitey and was out to get him and didn't care who got hurt as long as he got Whitey.

He offered to take care of the situation to show good faith and to send a message to anyone else who decided to go against the position of his group.

I thanked him for the offer but told him that I

would have to talk it over with my two partners and let him know in a few days. I wasn't sure whether we wanted to push this either way.

Shorty was all for having the guys in 'Pitt' send the two of them on an errand so that we could ambush them. Claude didn't want any part of that and was all for getting out of the business, period. Claude wasn't a coward, he just was not a violent man and felt that those guys would get paid whether we did it or not.

About a week and a half went by and before we could come to agreement I got a call from the main guy who told me that the two guys in question were missing. They found their car parked on a country road between here and Uniontown with nothing in it and the two guys hadn't been seen for over three or four days. He wanted to know if we knew anything and I told him that we had not decided and I doubted that we could. We agreed to keep each other posted and to continue with our business deal

We were sure that the group from 'Pitt' had handled the situation, if it had been handled at all, and they were covering their 'you know what'!

Anyway, we never heard anymore about it and we never saw those two 'yayhoos' again.

Chapter Sixteen

Things got back to normal except for Whitey being gone. I had to pick up on the things that he had done and it was a little hectic for a while. We were abele to convince Claude to stick it out for a while and to hire some help with the deliveries while the footballers were in season.

Shorty and I were sure that the stupid law would be repealed sooner or later and we would be sitting pretty to go legal. But it was not to be for us!

Business was good and the dough was coming in steady locally, as well as from 'Pitt'. We knew everbody you needed to know to survive because frankly, just about everybody did business with us from the local cops all the way to the state house. In fact, when the "Feds" first began to nose around, we would be told where they were going to be and when. We never lost a delivery or even had one of our trucks stopped by the locals or the federal treasury agents.

But the writin' was on the wall if you were payin' attention! Claude kept saying that he thought we were pushing our luck and we needed to ease out of the business. Shorty wanted to sell it to the guys in "Pitt". He felt we could hold out until we could work a deal because the locals would cover for us if the 'Feds' tried to by-pass them.

During one of our nose-to-nose talks I made the mistake of saying that If the 'Feds' did move in I would be the first one in line and would live with it! Claude came right back with 'I'll hold you to that'! Shorty didn't think it would come to that but said if it did he'd remember what I said!

One afternoon, your dad's cousin, the cop, came by the doughnut shop and had a cup of coffee and a "sinker". He seemed to take a little longer than usual and when the place didn't clear out to his liking he asked to see me in the back room. I was a little leary at first but I didn't have any reason not to trust him so we went in the back. He got right to the point and told me that the 'Feds' were putting the pressure on the Chief and he didn't know how long it would be until the Chief would have to decide whether to get on board or step aside. There wasn't any use to act like I didn't know what he was talking about because even he had been a customer more than once, and recently, at the time. I told him to tell the Chief not to put himself in hot water with the 'Feds' on my account and that whatever he decided to do, I would understand.

A few days later he was back and informed me that the Chief did not want to step aside for the 'Feds' because he was afraid that it would be opening the door for anything else they wanted to interfere with. The state police were willing to stay out of it if the Chief handled it. He also said that the Chief was sure that it would be better for me and my friends if he could keep this local. I agreed but stated that I would cooperate one hundred percent only if he could see of a way to leave my friends out of it. I was pretty sure that he didn't have anything concrete on Claude or Shorty because Whitey and I had been the ones out front all along and he would need my testimony to bring charges against either one of them.

I had talked to the guys in 'Pitt' to satisfy Shorty and they were getting the same pressure from the federals that we were. Their position was that they would do business as long as they could and weren't interested in buying us out.

As it turned out I agreed to signing off on the charges and shutting down the operation in return for a two year sentence in the state pen at Elkins, a heavy fine and some side payments which , along with the attorney fee for just standing up with me in court, wiped me out! Claude and Shorty promised to set me up when I got out and they kept their word, otherwise I couldn't have bought the roadhouse out on route #50. Two years didn't seem like too long a time then and if I hadn't cut a deal with the Chief I could have very likely ended up in a federal penitentiary for a minimum of five years along with Shorty and Claude. As it was, I was out in eighteen months. Like I said, Elkins wasn't bad after what you might call an orientation session because I knew a lot of the guys who were guards there. I took a pretty good beating a few nights after I got there before the guards broke it up because I didn't see myself as some bum's cotmate.

About a week after that, while out in the yard at break time, two guys came up to me and said the boss wanted to see me. Thinking that the warden wanted to see me I followed them across the yard to where this big moose was standing. When I stopped in front of him he said, 'Do you know who I am?' I said no but that I was told that the warden wanted to see me. Without another word he drove his fist into my jaw and I went down pretty hard. I wasn't out but it took me awhile before I could focus clearly. I had got to my knees by the time I could see okay and realized that he was standing in front of me with his feet apart and his hands on his hips. He said, 'That was just a sample of what I could expect in the future if I didn't fall in line because he was the boss of the yard!' A house didn't have to fall on me to let me know that if I rolled over for this guy my two years at Elkins would be pure hell!

I didn't even try to get up, I put a hard left and right straight into his 'nuts' from my knees. The left was a little off center but the right hit dead in 'where he lived'! He went down on his knees and I took my time to stand up and catch him along side of the neck with a solid right and he 'went sleepy nite-nite'.

The rest of my time at Elkins was as I told you. The 'boss' and I had an understanding that he could be the 'boss' all he wanted as long as it didn't include me! In fact, we even spoke or nodded to each other from time to time.

When I was released from Elkins, Claude and Shorty were waiting for me outside with an envelope and a set of keys to a new car. A lot of our relatives thought that they, and Whitey, were the reason for all of the trouble but I always knew that I was a big boy and was just as much, or more, to blame as anyone. Nobody ever made me do what I didn't want to! Anyway, except for what happened to Whitey, we used up a lot of luck and I couldn't have had better partners than what I had!

You want another beer "Britchy"?

When "Uncle Jamie" asked me if I wanted another beer I said no because I had seen that dad had returned from visiting Uncle Lee and other relatives, and was sitting out in the car waiting to head back to DC. Besides, I kind of lost count while he was telling me what he had to say and I had a pretty good "buzz" on by then! My emergency leave was up on Monday and I had to report back to Chelsea Naval Hospital, so I said goodbye to Aunt Vera, got in the car, and dad and I left for DC.

The drive back home to DC was nostalgic because we drove back on SR#50 through Mt. Storm and right by the roadhouse that looked like it wasn't being taken care of very well. As we went by my dad remarked that he didn't think that Jim and Vera were as happy now as they were at the roadhouse. He said that he got the impression that my uncle was reflecting too much on his previous life and asked what we talked about while he was visiting with Lee.

I told him that he might be right because "Unc" did all of the talking and I did the listening about his time in the business and how it all came to an end.

I said that he didn't seem to be bitter, just seemed to want to have someone hear his side of it, and maybe a little bit of hearing himself tell it too!

My dad replied that "Jim did ride high on the hog for quite awhile, but as they say, all good things come to an end, and usually from a direction you don't expect. Jim had it locked on the local and state level, but he and his pals didn't count on the "Feds" being able to turn the locals around and get them to do their work for 'em. They thought that the "Feds" would have to do it themselves and the locals would protect them while they had time to ease out with no losses. They didn't expect the state boys to step out of the way, either! Of course, as you probably know now, Jim is the one who took the loss!"

The rest of the drive home was pretty quiet because as I said before my dad wasn't much of a talker. We got home that evening, late, and I caught the train back to Boston early the next morning. Home wasn't the same without my mother and I still had a commitment to the Navy.

I would hear about "Unc" now and then from other members of the family. My cousin Glen told me that "Unc" wanted him to go into business with him when Glen got out of the Army and received his separation money. Glen said that he wasn't too keen on the idea because of "Unc"'s history and the fact that he was a little vague about what kind of business he had in mind.

With my mother gone and my sister married my dad asked me to come home when my hitch in the Navy was up so I did and went to work in construction as it was booming following the end of the war.

One day my dad told me that my uncle was in General Hospital in downtown DC and felt that I should go and see him as he had asked about me.

The next day I went down to the hospital to see him. He was his usual laid back, matter of fact self although I could tell that he was in a lot of pain. He told me that they were talking about taking one of his legs off because they couldn't stop the infection. He said that he didn't like that idea and wasn't sure he would go along with it. It was very similar to my mother's situation in that penicillin was still in the development stage primarily available to the military and somewhat limited to the public at the time. Medical treatment for the same conditions was much improved in a few short years after that.

We talked and he reminded me of a lot of the times we had when I visited him in the summers up in the mountains. He told me that I had in a lot of ways taken the place of his son Jimmy and he had enjoyed watching me grow and that I had made him proud more than once. I didn't ask him about the "proud business" because he might of clammed up right then and there, and I had a feeling he wanted to tell me something in particular.

I guess we talked for at least an hour when he said, "Britchy, do you remember the talk we had in Clarksburg after your mothers funeral?" I said yes but you did all of the talking. He replied, "Yeah, I was a real motor mouth wasn't I?" I waited for him to continue and he said, " Well, it's late in the game and I wanted to get something off my chest. Do you remember about the two guys from "Pitt" that we were sure did Whitey in and ended up missing just before I had to close the business down?" I said yes. "Well, the boys from "Pitt" thought that me, Shorty and Claude took care of those two guys and Claude and Shorty thought that they took care of them." He was quiet for a few seconds and then said, "I guess what I'm saying is that those two guys found a permanent home in the mountains for what they did to Whitey!" I noticed that he didn't say he did and he didn't say he didn't, and I didn't ask! I didn't know what to say!

Before I could say anything he said it was getting late and that I should get the hell out of there because a young single guy shouldn't be hanging around an old fart when there were good times to be had.

I told him that I wanted him to listen to his doctors because if he didn't he could die.

He looked at me and said. "Britchy, They told me that if I didn't quit drinking and smoking I would be dead in two years. Well if I quit drinking and smoking I might as well be dead in two years!"

And he was!

Uncle Jamie was born June 19, 1897. He died after having both legs amputated in an attempt to stop the infection that was taking over his body and was buried in the family plot in Clarksburg, West Virginia, in July of 1956.

He, along with my dad, taught me that there are no guarantees in life and to deal with what it handed me as best I could without griping.

When he heard that I had joined the Navy he told me to always keep my money in my socks and my socks on when participating in a one-night stand, because it is hard for someone to take your socks off without waking you up!

I admit that he said it with a subtle little grin that I had become used to over the years, but you have to admit that you can't get better advice than that!

Epiloge

My wife and I visited Clarksburg just prior to the publishing of this book as part of a vacation trip and as a matter of curiosity to see what changes had ocurred.

I found little change in the city proper except it was no easy task to go around the block when you missed a turn. You usually had to go around a number of blocks to go around the block! A few new buildings since I lived there as a boy, and a few that looked like they had been refurbished within recent times. Most of the expansion is outward as in most other cities in the country.

Monticello Avenue, where I lived, is understandably disappointing since my grandmothers house is gone as well as my uncle Lee's on the other side of the street, which was one of the group of houses that hung precariously over Elk Creek. A guard rail now exists where that group of houses was, which is a good idea. I can remember looking down on the creek from my uncle Lee's back porch. That was a view that one did not soon forget! I also remember getting my rear end "smoked" for playing in that creek which was, at that time, not the healthiest of activities.(My mother wasn't arrested for child abuse, I didn't play in the creek anymore, and I loved the ground she walked on!)

However, we found the people in Clarksburg just as friendly and helpful as always. While looking for my uncle's grocery store I struck up a conversation with a telephone repairman who had been raised in that particular neighborhood. He, and a very nice lady who was sweeping her sidewalk off, helped us realize that we were in the wrong part of town and that we should check with the public library to locate where the grocery store was.

Mr. Houchins, Director of the Geneology Department at the Clarksburg Public Library was most helpfull in locating and providing us with a copy of a 1952 City Directory, listing Gribble's Grocery on Traction Street.

Upon arriving in that neighborhood, I mistook the building on the corner of Traction and Liberty as my uncle's grocery store as it was quite similar to what I remembered.

My wife took a number of pictures of the building from different angles and I entered the barber shop, after I noticed that the two customers had finished their business and had left the shop, to introduce myself and explain our actions.

The owner of the shop, Mr. Ronald Mitchell, was most cordial and informative. He advised that his building was not the building that had housed Gribble's Grocery. His building, located at 897 Traction Street had previously housed Ware's Grocery and the barber shop. He stated that the barber shop was the oldest barber shop in the State of West Virginia in that it was 100 years old. The previous owner had operated it for 60 years and Mr. Mitchell had operated for the last 40 years. He took the time to point out the empty lot where Gribble's Grocery had been at 891 Traction on the corner of the alley down the block from Mr. Mitchell's building. It had been torn down two years before, after it was allowed to deteriorate by the owners and condemned by the city.

He stated that he had known my Aunt Vera who had been one of his wife's customers in her hair salon up until her death in 1984. Aunt Vera had kept the store after my uncle's death in 1956 until my cousin Glen found out that she was supporting it with her social security checks so the kids in the neighborhood would have a place to buy sodas and candy.

I knew that she had been robbed and assaulted by a young man in the neighborhood who had known her since he was a small boy. This happened long after my uncle's death and I was not told about it until she herself had passed on. The irony of it is that he assaulted a woman who, had he asked, might have given him the money. However, he is most fortunate to have been born too late to have met my uncle in his prime!

Having completed our mission in the neighborhood, my wife and I thanked Mr. Mitchell and proceeded out of Clarksburg on Rt # 50, east towards Mt. Storm.

We arrived in Mt. Storm a little after noon and found little change except the old church where I attended movie cartoons on Saturday night has been expanded into a much larger building, though it still looked like it might be used for church activities. The building that was the general store is all boarded up in the front. Except for that it still is a nice quiet little village.

The trip down the mountain to where the roadhouse used to be went quicker than I remembered and when the road leveled out in the valley I completely missed the fact that the road had been straightened out. We reached the other end of the valley before I realized that everything had changed. The old iron structured bridge has been replaced with a low profile concrete crossover and what used to be a river is hardley a creek on the south side of the highway. The north side flowed a lot better towards where I remembered the old mill to be. But I remembered also that there were large deep pools of water on that stretch of the river, bounded on both sides, by large boulders all the way to the old mill.

Slowing down to get a better look I noticed a gravel road on the northeast side of the crossover that followed the creek away from the highway. I turned into it since it was definitely not there before. I was curious as to where it went and soon found that two houses had been built on the east bank of what used to be the river. We passed the first house and pulled into the driveway of the second house which had a wide view of the creek from the backyard. Not wanting to trespass I went to the front door and a young man with his arm in a sling answered the bell. I introduced myself to him and he identified himself as Dale Davis. He was off work with a broken clavicle due to a motorcycle accident. Having had a few motorcycle accidents as well as a cracked clavicle, a gift from a big defensive tackle during a busted running play one night game, Dale and I found common ground pretty quickly. He gave my wife permission to take pictures of the creek from his back yard, cautioning her to watch for snakes, offered us a cold drink and was as gracious and hospitable as an individual could be who was obviously not too comfortable with his injury. He told us that the creek had cleared up quite a bit since they had moved into the house because the water had been almost orange from the spillage from the mines up the mountain on the other side of the highway.

He did say that the creek opened up more further down and described large pools of water similar to what I remembered. Since the road through the woods, in that direction, was not too inviting for a large conversion van and we did not feel comfortable looking for the owner to gain permission to trespass, we decided to forego visiting that area.

After a short but pleasant visit with Dale we drove back out to the highway and turned west back towards Mt. Storm in order to take a second look at the valley. We passed a house sitting in the spot where the large shaving pile used to be if we were still on the old road. Then I noticed the old road off to the left of us and turned in at the point where it intersected with the new. An entirely new/different building that looked like a maintenance structure of some kind sat approximately where the roadhouse had been. The property was posted so we made sure we honored that order.

Just before we were preparing to leave I noticed back on the right hand side of the property almost hidden in among the trees was a small building that was about the same size as one of the rental cabins, in approximately the same location as one that existed when the roadhouse was there. It was not in usable condition with the roof in poor shape and the window missing, including the sill down to the floor, to where part of a bed and discarded miscellaneous items were visable.

I can't be positive that it was one of the cabins but it sure looked like one of them!

Only part of the old road existed and as we drove back east on it to where it intersected with the new road, I noticed that the old church was gone and there wasn't one tree big eneough to be the old "bat" tree. It was as if the old woods had all died and new woods grew in place of them.

We continued east on Rt#50 until we reached what my family used to call the seven mile run. There you could look down into the valley where Abe Lincoln's mother, Nancy Hanks, was born and raised.

At one point the mountains across the valley look like a saddle and at another point they resemble a cradle.

I received another surprise at the point where you begin the descent down the mountain because a pullover and parking area with a telescope on a concrete pedestal next to a small gift shop now existed where none existed before. A sign proclaiming the area as "Saddle Mountain" and listing pertinent information was posted prominently. My sister and I had to find out all of that information from our mother who was the family authority on West Virginia lore.

As we continued on down the mountain I couldn't help reflecting on how much the valley that I had enjoyed so much as a boy had changed. No roadhouse, no shaving pile, no church, no bat tree, and most of all, no river!

Thomas Wolfe sure knew what he was talking about when he wrote, "You can't ever go home again!" Or something like that!

The End

Printed in the United States
2734